Leaders in Development

Leaders in Development:
Enhancing Your Leadership Effectiveness in a Changing World

May 2, 2017
Copyright © 2017 by Center for Asia Leadership Initiatives
Printed in Seoul, Korea

A Publication of the Center for Asia Leadership Initiatives
Acumen Publishing
14 Nancy Lane Waltham MA 02452 USA

Center for Asia Leadership Initiatives
Website: www.asialeadership.org
Facebook: www.facebook.com/asiagroup

Asia Leadership Trek
Website: www.asialeadershiptrek.org
Facebook: www.facebook.com/asialeadershiptrek
Twitter & Weibo: @Asia_Trek

All rights reserved. No part of this book may be reprinted or reproduced or utilized in any form or by any electronic mechanical, or other means, now known or hereafter invented, including photocopying and recording, or in any information storage or retrieval system, without permission in writing from the publisher.

Library of Congress Control Number 2017938472
KDP ISBN: 979-8-6399177-6-9
US $10.99

For inquiries on partnership or sponsorship, or purchase of the publication, please email us at: cali@asialeadership.org

Cover design courtesy of Jin-ok Heo
Typesetting Courtesy of Chun-hee Lee

Leaders in Development

Enhancing Your Leadership Effectiveness
in a Changing World

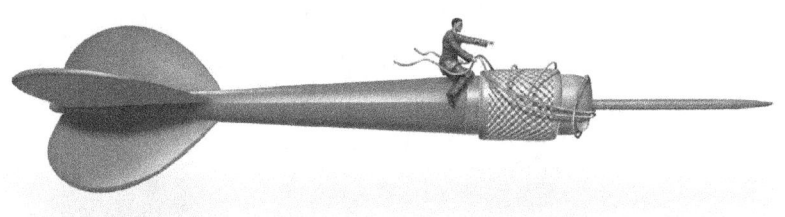

*10 Professionals Share Key Insights and Inspiration
on Leading Change in Asia*

edited by Hungsoo S. Kim

ACUMEN™
PUBLISHING

To all the aspiring leaders of this world

| Table of Contents |

•••

About the Editor   9
About the Contributors   11
Foreword   15

Introduction

| Introduction | Set Yourself Apart and Get Ahead of the Curve

_ **Hungsoo S. Kim**   19

Part 1 • History and Philosophy

| Chapter 1 | Transition from ALT to ALI: Boston to Malaysia

_ **Hungsoo S. Kim**   29

| Chapter 2 | Leadership Matters

_ **Dr. Gin Chee Tong**   35

Part 2 • Case Method Teaching: A Way Forward for Effective Pedagogy

| Chapter 3 | Journey to the World of Case Method of Teaching: From Analysis to Synthesis

_ **Dr. Cordelia Mason** 51

| Chapter 4 | Seek First to Understand

_ **Dr. Hendry Ng** 71

Part 3 • Personal Leadership: Ethics, Power, and Decision Making

| Chapter 5 | The Ethics of Deciding between People and Rules

_ **Elma Berisha** 91

| Chapter 6 | First Impressions—Lasting Impact: A Hard Lesson in Humility

_ **Yasmin M. Handrich** 109

| Chapter 7 | My Leadership Journey

_ **Peter K.H. Law** 129

Part 4 • Community Leadership: Leading Change for Organizational Renewal

| Chapter 8 | Leveraging Uncertainty and Unlocking Your Best Self

_ **Ida Fazila Ismail** 149

| Chapter 9 | A Bangladeshi Tale of Digital Dilemmas

_ **Sheikh Mohammed Irfan** 171

| Chapter 10 | A Muslim Woman's Success and Failures in Leadership

_ **Shamza Khan** 185

| Chapter 11 | Making This World a Better Place Through "Knowing, Doing, and Being"

_ **Katherine Kee** 201

Editor's Acknowledgments	211
Appendix I: Program Details	215
Appendix II: About the Teaching Faculty	223
Appendix III: List of Contributors	229

| About the Editor |

•••

Hungsoo S. Kim, a Korean national, is the Co-founder and President of the Center for Asia Leadership Initiatives. Passionate about nurturing and empowering talents in Asia, he has been actively engaging various stakeholders in developing and running over twenty-five programs in more than twenty-two countries in Asia to help emerging leaders explore opportunities to be socially responsible in facing the region's complex challenges. These programs fall under the Center's four main initiatives, namely the Asia Leadership Trek, a public diplomacy arm for scholars at Harvard, Stanford, MIT, and Fletcher; the Asia Leadership Institute, a leadership capacity-building arm; the Acumen Case Center, a research and content development arm; and Acumen Publishing, a publication arm. Hungsoo oversees these initiatives, along with a team of twenty comprising Faculty and Teaching Fellows from Harvard and Stanford University, and administrators at the main office in Boston, U.S., and the Asian regional headquarters in Kuala Lumpur, Malaysia.

As part of his continuous endeavor toward grooming leaders of tomorrow, Hungsoo recently joined the Asia Future Institute, a Seoul-based policy and leadership think tank, as Executive Director to instill in Korean and Northeast Asian talents the drive and passion to create positive social change through effective leadership. He prides himself on accelerating efforts to reach out to all forty-eight countries in Asia by 2022. Hungsoo's areas of research and training, among others, include 'Negotiation and Mediation,' 'Adaptive Leadership,' 'Persuasion and Influence,' and 'Creative Confidence.' To date, some twenty-five thousand burgeoning and established leaders from the government, non-profits, and corporate world in Asia have benefited from these programs.

Prior to establishing the Center, Hungsoo worked for twelve years in varying sectors from strategy consulting and social entrepreneurship to international development, politics, and government. He has also served as a policy aide in the United Nations in New York representing Korea, and as a project analyst at UNESCO in Paris. He currently sits on the board of two non-profit organizations, and has served as a visiting scholar at the Asia Center at Harvard University and at the Kellogg School of Management in Northwestern University. Hungsoo holds a Masters of Public Administration from the Harvard Kennedy School of Government; Masters in International Cooperation from the Graduate School of International Studies, Seoul National University; and completed his undergraduate studies with two majors in U.S. and International Law, and International Politics with a minor in Economics from Handong University.

Previously, Hungsoo was the editor of four books, namely *Rethinking Asia Vol. 1: Education and Innovation*, *Rethinking Asia Vol. 2: Entrepreneurship and Economic Development*, *Finding the Leaders in Us: New Goals for the Future*, and *Redefining Success: Learning to Lead for Change*. He is the editor of three upcoming books scheduled for release in May entitled, *Rethinking Asia Vol. 3: Social and Political Change*, *Next Generation Leadership: Empower Youth to Shape the Future of Asia*, and *Leaders in Development: Enhancing Your Leadership Effectiveness in a Changing World*.

| About the Contributors |

•••

Hungsoo S. Kim is the Co-founder and President of the Center for Asia Leadership Initiatives. Passionate about nurturing and empowering talents in Asia, he has developed and organized over twenty-five programs in more than twenty-two countries in the region to help budding leaders enhance their leadership competencies to navigate challenges in the 21st century. Hungsoo aims to engage with youth in all forty-eight countries in Asia by 2022 and inspire them to enact change in the world.

Dr. Gin Chee Tong is the Head of Strategy & Management at the Center for Asia Leadership Initiatives (CALI) in Malaysia. She has previously worked in corporate communications, public relations, and tertiary education. An ardent student of the humanities, she graduated with a Bachelor of Arts (Media & Communications) (Honours) in 2005, and received her Doctorate of Philosophy (PhD) from the University of Melbourne, Australia in 2012. Dr Tong counts her family as her biggest supporters and sources of inspiration. When she is not at work, she can be found nose-deep in books, or traipsing halfway across the globe in search of new experiences.

Dr. Cordelia Mason works as a Research Fellow at Asian Institute of Finance. She is currently an Associate Fellow of the Malaysian Institute of Management and a member of the Board of Examiners for the Asian Institute of Chartered Bankers. She has three decades of experience in academia and has assumed positions as a lecturer, deputy dean, and dean. Dr. Mason enjoys writing and has written three textbooks for the Malaysian school system, quality manuals, lyrics for UniKL and Akademi Infotech MARA songs, curriculum manuals for business and management programs, twelve revisions books, storyboards, journal articles, as well as case studies. A self-professed informal knowledge broker, she is ever-willing to share what little she knows, and is constantly trying to discover new ways of learning.

Dr. Hendry Ng is the Director for the Victoria University Postgraduate Programmes at Sunway College, Malaysia. He holds a Bachelor's Degree in Computer Science, from the Royal Melbourne Institute of Technology, Australia; a Master of Business Administration (MBA) from Maastricht School of Management, Netherlands; and a Doctor of Business Administration (DBA) from Charles Sturt University, Australia. He started his career as a software engineering in 1983 before joining academia in 1991, where he taught and administered transnational higher education programs in private institutions of higher education.

Elma Berisha works for the Kuala Lumpur-based Asian Institute of Finance as General Manager for Strategy, Policy Development & Research. Prior to this, Elma was Regional Manager for Consumer Research and Public Perceptions in Asia Pacific at Frost & Sullivan, the global consulting company specialized in growth strategy. She has been involved in the study of public perceptions in Malaysia and Singapore, monitoring in particular issues of public safety, corruption, and urban development. Her insightful inputs on areas to improve from the perspective of public perceptions have directly contributed to the enhancement of the Performance Management and Delivery Unit (PEMANDU) project teams' monitoring of the Government Transformation Program (GTP).

Yasmin M. Handrich is a quirky, energetic, charming, and quick witted German living in Malaysia for the past fifteen years. She has eight years of consulting and market research experience across the Technology, Media, Telecommunications, and Financial Services sectors under her belt.

Peter K.H. Law has more than twenty years of commercial experience in the Services and Financial Services sectors. He is passionate about people development and believes in authentic leadership. He is also a certified coach and dedicates his time to developing youth for both the public and private sectors for the betterment of the community and country.

Ida Fazila Ismail studied insects at university, but switched to developing a career in public relations upon graduation. Today, she devotes her professional time to writing. A proud introvert, Ida wishes to one day immerse herself in the quiet solitude of Tasmania's wilderness.

Sheikh Mohammed Irfan is a passionate Bangladeshi entrepreneur who specializes in the technological industry. He thrives on innovation and the development of pragmatic solutions for emerging markets. His areas of expertise include system architecture, Fintech, the Internet of Things (IoT), big data, machine learning, data science, semantics, and cyber security. He aspires to enable and bridge the development of technological markets and the construction of decentralized platforms for the masses, with the empowerment of the youth. His work focuses on capacity building, consultancy, advocacy, innovation, and leadership. He is the Co-founder of the technology startup, Cyber Giant Systems Inc.; Founder of BD Fintech, a Bangladeshi Fintech Platform; Co-founder of Digital Value Holdings, a global Fintech initiative led by Massachusetts Institute of Technology (MIT) cohorts; Co-founder of Cyberia Academy, a technology education startup; Editor and Co-founder of *DOHS Times*, a community-based web news portal; and member of the Singapore Fintech Association, Global IoT Association, among other things. He has a multidisciplinary background and received education and training in the fields of Robotics Engineering, Data Science, System Engineering, and Financial Technology from institutions including Manchester Metropolitan University (MMU) and MIT.

Shamza Khan is a case writer and author for distinguished universities such as Columbia University and Harvard University. She has published over twenty Asia-focused business and marketing case studies listed in the prestigious *Harvard Business Review*. Most recently, she co-authored *Marketing Principles: Asia Edition* with Noel Capon.

Katherine Kee is the Manager for Public Relations at Sunway Education Group, looking into media relations and content creation for media releases. Before her current position in the education sector, she has worked in various industries including retail, healthcare, hospitality, advertising, and information technology. Born and raised in Penang, Katherine moved to Kuala Lumpur at the end of 1999.

| Foreword |

•••

With the advent of new information technologies, the world is becoming more globalized than ever. Globalization has shrunk the influence of time and geography by the click of a mouse. Everyone is interdependent and interconnected with each other regardless of our culturally diverse world.

Asia boasts an economically robust region, brimming with a vibrant ethnic diversity not found in other parts of the world. As the balance of economic power is shifting from West to East, the world recognizes that the lion's share of the history of the 21st century will be written in Asia.

Having said that, enormous opportunities lie ahead for leaders in Asia to create significant change. It would be a shame to not seize these opportunities. However, leaders need to acknowledge that they need a new set of skills to manage the challenges in today's ever-evolving world. Agile leaders of the 21st century have no choice but to gain the ability to adapt to rapidly changing environments and to work well across different cultures if they want to survive in the long run.

I applaud the Center for Asia Leadership Initiatives (CALI) for offering comprehensive leadership programs that emphasize the essential skills needed to be an effective leader in today's challenging world. I am pleased to be given the opportunity to work together with CALI in one of its leadership programs in Malaysia, namely "Community Leadership: Leading Change for Organizational Renewal." I am glad to have shared my knowledge with the delegates who came from various professional backgrounds. I hope that they have benefitted from my program, and gained knowledge on the importance of developing crucial skills to be an agent of change.

I believe the reflections written by a diverse group of professionals that are presented in this book will give readers unique and interesting perspectives on realizing their full potential as successful leaders. Leaders regardless of their career fields need to understand that in a world that knows no boundaries, power is widely distributed and no single person is "all-powerful." Everyone has some power to influence people's mindsets and complex systems. Therefore, a leader must identify actions that harness diverse power networks to foster creativity and analytical thinking in problem solving and decision making.

In the past, society tended to focus excessively on the personalities and characteristics of great leaders, not the context or process. They assumed that with the right talents, a leader could lead in any situation. The flaws in the previous models of leadership sparked my interest to embark on the development and teaching of adaptive leadership. Leaders who are able to adapt their approach in any context are more capable of dealing more positively with change. In order to mobilize people to embrace change, a leader must strive to create conditions that facilitate learning so that people will understand why change is needed to respond quickly and effectively in tackling complex challenges.

Asia is progressing at such a fast pace. Successful leaders are those who are willing to get out of their comfort zone and learn continuously to adapt to changed circumstances. The region has a lot of talented people. If they are prepared to take risks and implement innovative strategies for the future, I am confident that their leadership will greatly impact the fortunes of Asia.

Professor Dean Williams
Adjunct Lecturer in Public Policy for the Center for Public Leadership
Harvard Kennedy School

Introduction

| Introduction |

Set Yourself Apart and Get Ahead of the Curve

Hungsoo S. Kim
MPA, Harvard Kennedy School of Government

● ● ●

Poor leadership in organizations is all too common, regardless of whether you are in Asia, Europe, or the United States. Why does this happen? The answer is simply that the world has many bosses but few leaders. How do we solve this issue? First, we need to differentiate between leaders and bosses: bosses are managers who command their subordinates, while leaders demonstrate ethical values and inspire their colleagues to step out of their comfort zones. Leaders know how to get the most out of people and foster an environment that develops the full potential of others. Most importantly, leaders know that they must continuously enhance and expand their leadership skills in order to contribute effectively to their organizations and communities.

People are leaders' most valuable assets, and thus leaders should leverage and maximize their employees' contributions to increase the overall success of their organizations. Leaders must be able to harness the full potential of their employees and encourage them to create positive change by creating an environment conducive to lifelong learning and sustainable personal development.

Anyone who has ever led a team knows that leadership is not always smooth sailing. Even the most charismatic leaders encounter setbacks in their careers, but—despite the inevitable obstacles—good leaders never give up and always keep their eyes on their goals. One of the greatest examples that exemplifies persistence in leadership is Abraham Lincoln. He lost eight elections, twice failed in business, and suffered a nervous breakdown before becoming President of the United States. Today's leaders must be similarly persistent, pushing boundaries, and motivating people to buy into a common vision and make things better. They must also keep their egos in check, to avoid going down the slippery slope toward poor leadership.

Effective leadership is crucial in adapting organizations and communities to the exponential shifts occurring in our globalized world. The world is becoming ever more interconnected, complex, and volatile. Everything is moving at a tremendous rate, and we will be left behind if we are not well-equipped to meet the challenges of the 21st century. The recent U.S. presidential election and the Brexit vote highlighted this risk, in which the two events indicate a powerful, worldwide trend toward nationalism, protectionism, and de-globalization. I anticipate increased uncertainties in the upcoming year, but only time will tell how the future will unfold in Asia.

Asia is a dynamic region with a thriving economy and rapid trade growth. The rise of China and India as economic powerhouses and the emergence of other Asian countries as key players in regional and global markets will shape the 21st century. In light of these challenges, we need a new breed of leaders, ones who understand the complexity of the world's most pressing issues, including economic instability and social inequality, and are committed to making a positive impact. It is imperative for Asia, as one of the world's most powerful regions, to promote sustainable development and to contribute to shared prosperity, with leaders who not only recognize the interdependence between Asia and the world, but can also adapt to ever-evolving global circumstances. Acknowledging these necessities will allow them to analyze current issues and emerging trends, identify opportunities, and tackle challenges from different perspectives. With these skills, essential in sparking breakthrough ideas and solutions, our leaders will be able to think outside the box, and explore fresh insights and approaches to today's challenges.

We are on the brink of the Fourth Industrial Revolution, which will fundamentally change the way we live and work. Organizations will have no choice but to innovate and adapt to these changes in order to stay ahead of the competition, facing the headwinds caused by disruptive technologies such as artificial intelligence, big data, co-existent reality (CR), 3D printing, biotechnology, robotics, and new forms of money. All of these inventions will significantly impact leadership styles and organizational operations. Our leaders, therefore, must redefine leadership in order to stay relevant in this fast-moving, fickle, and ambiguous environment. It all boils down to change: organizations must either disrupt or get disrupted. They must stay on their toes, seizing opportunities by empowering their workforce, reinventing the way things work, and creating innovative approaches for every new change.

At the Center for Asia Leadership Initiatives (CALI), we understand the importance of cultivating new leaders, as every generation must face the opportunities and responsibilities of its own era. Since its establishment in Cambridge, Massachusetts, in early 2014, to its move to the

Asian headquarters in Kuala Lumpur, Malaysia, the following year, CALI remains committed to bringing the Harvard way of developing leaders and leadership to Asian communities. Leveraging the resources and exceptional teaching faculty of Harvard, our Center aims to provide effective and innovative solutions for personal leadership development at both the organizational and the community levels. Our goal is to create societal leaders who will enact affirmative change in their communities. In line with CALI's philosophy of "knowing, doing, and being," we encourage leaders to make the most of what they have for the benefit of others. "Knowing" refers to the knowledge that one acquires throughout life; "doing" refers to turning knowledge into action in order to help other people; while "being" refers to developing self-awareness, which in turn helps others fulfill their own potential.

CALI has established several initiatives to address 21st century leadership challenges. One of them is the Asia Leadership Institute (ALI), which offers Asia Leadership Executive (ALE) programs to professionals, managers, and senior leadership from the government, civil society, and business realms, as well as giving aspiring youth access to world-class talent development programs, leadership training, and specialized educational experiences. In 2016, ALI completed three major ALE programs under the Global Change Agents banner; they received a strong positive response from the participating professionals, who came from countries all around the world, including Bangladesh, Germany, Korea, Japan, Kosovo, Macedonia, Malaysia, Pakistan, Singapore, and the United States.

In August, we organized the first two of these programs, in which each ran for five days: "Personal Leadership: Ethics, Power, and Decision Making" and "Case Method Teaching: A Way Forward for Effective Pedagogy," both with Professor Mathias Risse and Professor Kenneth Winston from the Harvard Kennedy School of Government (HKS). The "Personal Leadership" program aimed to help working professionals strategically improve their personal leadership and gain core competencies to solve complex organizational issues. During the program, participants learned how to broaden their perspectives in all domains, becoming more effective and accountable in their personal values, and their professional ethical standards. The "Case Method Teaching" program exposed participants to the case method employed at the Harvard Business, Medical, and Kennedy Schools. The method is an inventive educational approach that places students in the roles of decision makers, allowing them to address some of the greatest challenges confronting today's companies, non-profits, and government organizations. Together, these two ALE programs used fourteen Harvard case studies to spark lively discussions and facilitate self-reflection in sixty-five participants.

Following the success of these two programs, we introduced a three-day "Community Leadership: Leading Change for Organizational Renewal" program in October, led by Professor Dean Williams, Adjunct Lecturer in Public Policy for the Center for Public Leadership, HKS. The program guided working professionals toward acquiring the skills and knowledge needed to encourage regeneration at the workplace. It addressed the crucial need for organizations to be agile and innovative in order to compete in rapidly changing business environments. The participants also explored an adaptive leadership framework that fosters creative thinking and flexibility in the workplace. This framework, taught in one of the most popular courses at HKS, inspires leaders to become change agents, to cross boundaries, and to build bridges, creating strong relationships with relevant stakeholders in order to tackle challenges effectively.

This book offers reflections by nine participants of the abovementioned programs, giving readers a glimpse into their experiences of acquiring new leadership skills. Readers will discover how our programs inspired the participants to take positive actions in their professional and personal lives. I commend these ten participants for taking time out of their busy schedules to share their journeys with us. I feel confident that this book will incite readers' own inner drives to enact change and improve lives in today's complex world.

The book is divided into three parts. In Part 1, you will first find a chapter by me, explaining CALI's transition from its flagship initiative, the Asia Leadership Trek (ALT), to the ALI and its ALE programs. You will find out in this chapter what spurred our idea to develop programs that promote effective leadership among working professionals. Dr. Gin Chee Tong will then delve into her experience in one of ALE's earlier workshops, which showed her that leadership is a skill that can be taught and learned. Her chapter lays the foundation for the book, giving an overview of what our ALE programs have to offer.

Part 2 features reflections from participants of the "Case Method Teaching" program. In Chapter 3, Dr. Cordelia Mason invites readers to think critically about ethical issues with the aim of refining their moral compasses in today's ever-changing environment. She explains how the case study method taught her invaluable lessons in exploring different perspectives. In Chapter 4, Dr. Hendry Ng highlights the importance of understanding our surroundings before taking action, in order to seek clarification and to obtain the best results in our professional and personal lives. He writes about his experience at an institution of higher learning in Malaysia as an example of how one's personal moral values can collide with one's professional codes of ethics.

Part 3 comprises insights from the "Personal Leadership" program. It opens with a chapter by Elma Berisha of Kosovo, who has built a successful career in Malaysia and at one point, realized the need to strike a balance between upholding an ethical principle and preserving her relationships with those around her. In this chapter, readers will discover how the ALE program transformed Elma's way of thinking about rules and principles. Chapter 6 was written by Yasmin M. Handrich, a young German professional in Malaysia, who describes how an individual's moral principles can play a vital role in managing ethical crises at the workplace. In Chapter 7, Peter K.H. Law reflects on how discussions with professors and participants of the ALE programs taught him how to tackle ethical challenges, both personally and professionally.

Part 4 consists of chapters by professionals who attended the "Community Leadership" program. It begins with Ida Fazila Ismail's chapter on how the program reshaped the way she thinks about leadership; she argues that everyone can make a difference regardless of their circumstances, and she illustrates key points from the program through real-life stories that resonate with her. Her chapter encourages readers to look at tough times as opportunities to reflect and grow, and to develop adaptability and gratitude in the face of adversity. In Chapter 9, Sheikh Mohammed Irfan covers his passion for technological entrepreneurship and the many challenges he has faced in his home country of Bangladesh. He examines his new understanding of leadership following his participation in the program, which prompted him to reflect on his past decisions and to think of new ways to enhance his leadership skills. Irfan stresses the need to look within when addressing challenges and opportunities, and to take ownership of our actions instead of relying on others to change the world. Chapter 10 was written by Shamza Khan, a Pakistani Muslim woman who grew up in the British education system in Hong Kong and then embarked on a career in the U.S. The chapter follows her transformational leadership journey and offers key takeaways from the program. Shamza wants readers to know that every little bit counts when inspiring change within ourselves and in the world. Lastly, Katherine Kee in Chapter 11, ponders how to be a contributing member of society and to generate change through one's job. She reveals how the ALE program encouraged her to develop leadership qualities and to inspire other people in their quests for change. Her chapter includes personal and professional stories of effective leadership that demonstrate CALI's concepts of "knowing, doing, and being."

I encourage all the readers of this book to seek a greater sense of purpose as they lead their organizations and communities into the future. In order to exercise effective leadership, we must maintain respect, humility, and honor, and we must always strive to contribute to the betterment of mankind. When managing challenges, we must stand "on the balcony" to look at the big picture and view our situation from different perspectives. We must also spend time "on the dance floor" to learn firsthand about the conditions in our civic groups, organizations, and communities. Above all, we must never stop learning, and seeking new knowledge and skills from others.

Happy reading, and I wish you all the best in your leadership quest!

Part 1

History and Philosophy

| Chapter 1 |

Transition from ALT to ALI:
Boston to Malaysia

Hungsoo S. Kim

● ● ●

It was August 18, 2014, nine in the morning. Months of planning and countless hours spent poring over applications have led to the Center for Asia Leadership Initiatives' (CALI) first week-long leadership program in Malaysia with participants from a diverse range of backgrounds and future trajectories. From private sector and government to the educational and non-profit sectors, a great blend of promising and emerging young professionals had convened to embark on a journey that would steer them to become effective agents of change in their respective communities. I took pride in what lay ahead for this group as our previous leadership programs set a high bar, which I am convinced we could meet if not surpass.

Establishing the Asia Leadership Executive (ALE) program came naturally from the ongoing success of the Asia Leadership Trek (ALT) and its brainchild, the Asia Leadership Institute (ALI). The former was a program that offered a month-long trek across multiple countries in Asia which gave scholars from Harvard University, Massachusetts Institute of Technology (MIT), and Tufts Fletcher School of Law and Diplomacy the opportunity to acquire firsthand insights through an experiential journey, in which the participants directly investigated the challenges and opportunities of each country through engagement with its key decision makers and thought leaders. The highlight of this program, I must say, was the aspect in which the participants engaged in knowledge dissemination, or in our own terms, 'giving back to the community' in the form of providing mentorship, sharing inspirational stories on leadership, leading discussions on best practices, as well as executing capacity building workshops on the topics of leadership, innovation, and entrepreneurship with the communities. These two elements came about as part of a wider goal of experiencing and discovering, yet also making a meaningful impact in various corners of Asia.

It is noteworthy that it was only through this latter aspect that the ALI was brought forth. Consequently, due to its sweeping growth both in the scope of its activity and reach, the ALI, an organization that worked solely on providing scores of cutting edge leadership training, specialized education, and academic and cultural experiences, was greatly needed to serve different communities in Asia.

Among the many programs we introduced was the ALE. Multiple factors contributed to its development. In many places in Asia like Malaysia, the demand for effective public leadership has never been greater. Malaysia in particular, with its nervy economy coupled with the liberalization of certain key sectors in recent years has cemented its need for capable and visionary individuals who are able to unlock the country's full potential. The continuous calibration and refinement of our teaching practices across Asia has given us the technical expertise to conduct educational tracks of greater breadth and depth.

Through discussions with John Lim, Managing Director of CALI Boston and my trusted friend who served alongside me at the Center, we agreed that a specific program was needed to cater to young professionals who were willing to learn, push themselves, and ultimately serve the nation in their various capacities. Speaking of the ALE in Malaysia, three ingredients were vital for its success: firstly, the unconventional program or contents that we had brought into the region; secondly, the caliber and the level of commitment of the participants; and lastly, the quality of the Teaching Faculty and Fellows. The combination would prove to be an enriching experience for those teaching and those learning, two functions that were eagerly blurred and pursued simultaneously throughout the duration.

Since the first ALE program in 2014, CALI has organized five more programs in Malaysia: two in 2015 and three in 2016. This book showcases personal essays of the program participants in which you will discover their goals and life purpose through their reflections. The participants shared something in common – their willingness to take up the responsibility to face challenging times, and to identify the opportunities as well as to brainstorm and develop plans that can turn downsides into upsides. They came united by this mutual desire to make Malaysia a better place, believing that they had a unique opportunity and responsibility to contribute and make a difference.

We were privileged to have the CALI Teaching Faculty and Fellows to conduct workshops for the participants. They brought with them a wealth of experience from their respective fields and their often illustrious backgrounds. More importantly, they had a strong desire to give back to the community in a way that is impactful at the very heart of society—human capital. Coming from various backgrounds, from education and military to consulting, finance, and diplomacy, they did an amazing job, in particular, engaging the delegates in thinking about the kind of Malaysia they wanted to create years from now, to share thoughts on what and how they could be a linchpin to their country's success and prosperity, and to contribute in their best capacities in order to face and solve the challenges they saw at hand.

Good teachers and mentors are indispensable. Of the many lessons I have learned throughout life, mostly I have gleaned from leaders I have come to know in my professional and sometimes personal capacity. My first job started right after college. I was given an opportunity to work as a political advisor at the United Nations in New York. Besides gaining firsthand exposure to the diverse international security matters affecting our world, working with many inspiring Foreign Service leaders left an indelible impression on the importance of engaging with the great leaders of the world. Among many I came across, was one diplomat who would spend hours every week preparing personal handwritten thank you notes to fellow diplomats he had worked closely with. One politician I served under, once took time out of his busy schedule just because a group of students came to the office unannounced to take a picture with him. It is their personal edge and sacrificial character that set them apart—the very same traits I observe in our Teaching Faculty and Fellows.

The popularity of the ALE is perhaps obvious as it, in many ways mirrors the attractiveness of the ALT. In the ALT, the Trekkers were drawn to the opportunities presented for community service, mutual learning, as well as intellectual exposure and growth through close proximity interactions with current and up-and-coming leaders. Likewise, participants of the ALE were able to draw from the success of the Teaching Faculty and Fellows who have dedicated their lives to service that brings good to the public. The pool of participants also meant that they were able to engage in exchange of ideas, working practices, and innovative solutions to pressing issues. Through the interactive elements of the program, they were able to leverage on the successes and failures of their fellow peers in striving toward betterment. Finally, participants were exposed to cutting edge research in the field of leadership, giving them only the best resources, which is vital in helping them to navigate today's fast-paced and globalized world.

But beyond the personal benefits the ALE has to offer, my hope is that participants will be inspired by its underlying rationale—"ask not what the country can do for you, but ask what you can do for your country," as once said by John F. Kennedy. Having witnessed how powerful ideas and strong guiding expertise can have on real-world applications, and how a strong sense of passion and idealism can bring meaningful change to our society, I want all those who spent many of their invaluable hours attending the ALE to eventually learn that "nothing great will ever be achieved without great men, and men are great only if they are determined to be so"—Charles de Gaulle. I hope that all our efforts will pay off by seeing many people becoming effective and ethical leaders who are determined to achieve something great for the community. Let's work together to inspire those around us toward growth in leadership and social change.

| Chapter 2 |

Leadership Matters

Dr. Gin Chee Tong

• • •

Can Leadership Be Learned?

On December 2, 1986, *The New York Times* published an article by Daniel Goleman with the headline "Major Personality Study Finds That Traits Are Mostly Inherited." One of the traits cited as being most strongly determined by heredity was leadership, underlining the commonly held belief that "leaders are not made, they are born." Fast forward to the 21st century, and we have J. E. De Neve's 2012 study, which argued that leaders' brains are "wired differently from most," as they have "more grey matter in places that control decision making and memory, giving them a vital edge when it comes to making the right call."[1] This idea that DNA determines one's leadership

---

1 De Neve, J. E. *et al* (2013) 'Born to lead? A twin design and genetic association study of leadership role occupancy', *The Leadership Quarterly* 24, 45–60.

skills may dishearten many aspiring leaders. If we did not inherit the so-called "leadership gene," can we still learn to be good leaders?

The short answer is a resounding yes, if one goes by the ALE programs organized by CALI's ALI for working professionals. Through interactive workshops, professional development sessions and small-group discussions facilitated by Teaching Fellows from Harvard University and Stanford University, the ALE programs dismiss the notion that only those in management positions qualify as leaders. Instead, they promote the theory that leadership is a skill that can be taught and learned.

In the workshop "Transformational Leadership," led by Mr. Adam Malaty-Uhr of the Harvard Graduate School of Education, he explained that there are two types of authority: the first, formal authority describes a position of decision making; the second, informal authority refers to a position of influence conferred on us by the group. To demonstrate this difference, he invited workshop participants to create a list of standard behaviors for the entire class. Because we perceived Mr. Malaty-Uhr as having formal authority, our initial response was to wait for him to provide suggestions. Our reaction was by no means unusual; in most Asian educational settings, students wait passively for information to be given to them by the teacher. However, when it became clear that he had no plans to provide direction—he had, in fact, taken a seat and was busily scribbling into his notebook—one of the delegates stood up and began inviting other delegates to give suggestions, thus taking on a position of informal authority. This exercise made it clear that leadership is fundamentally a choice, not a position.

Sometimes we can decide for ourselves whether we want to take on a leadership role; at other times, the leadership role is conferred, regardless of whether we are ready to accept it or not. To demonstrate this, we need to only think of the role of a parent or of someone recently promoted to a managerial position. While the former may seem self-selected and the latter an outcome determined by external forces, the reverse may be equally true. We may be unexpectedly thrust into a position of parental authority or fight for the responsibility to lead a team. Through the ALE programs, we come to learn the mantle of leadership may come to us at any point. If we want to achieve the best outcome for ourselves, our families, and our communities, good leadership is fundamental.

What then are the defining qualities of a good leader? From what I observed through the ALE programs, I believe a good leader is someone who chooses to speak up, who seeks to create value for everyone, and who understands that leadership cannot be exercised alone.

"The Only Wrong Question is the Question Not Asked"

In many cultures, particularly those in Asia, speaking up is often misconstrued as being arrogant or disrespectful, particularly if the listener is older or holds a higher position than the speaker. The popular saying that "children should be seen, not heard" is constantly drummed into young learners' minds. It is therefore not unusual to hear people confess to having little confidence in speaking up, as they were worried about saying "something stupid." However, as we were constantly reminded throughout the leadership programs, speaking up is a crucial part of effective and efficient leadership, necessary in communicating and clarifying directions, informing people of expectations and goals, and uniting and motivating others. If we choose to stifle our thoughts for fear of being wrong, we risk putting everyone in situations where mistakes may be left unacknowledged or the work becomes inefficient due to a lack of direction. As Ms. Rachel Roberts from the Harvard Graduate School of Education puts it, "The only wrong question is the question not asked."

That said, voicing our thoughts aloud is not enough to make us effective leaders, nor will it guarantee that others will think or act differently. To get people to change their minds and behaviors, Mr. John Lee from the Harvard Kennedy School told us that leaders must learn to speak persuasively. When leaders are persuasive influencers, they can have a positive impact in the workplace, motivating peers and colleagues to pursue not just personal developments but organizational improvement. Consider powerful speakers such as Mahatma Gandhi, Oprah Winfrey, and Nick Vujicic, each has used public speaking to inspire people to break boundaries and overcome challenges.

To demonstrate the power of persuasive speaking, we were given the task of pitching a topic of our choice to a large audience, using persuasion as the key element. Mr. Lee explained that the primary rationale for the exercise came from his experience at Harvard, where many students from Asia performed poorly due to lack of class participation. This motivated Mr. Lee to teach public speaking, with the hope of showing students that speaking persuasively and confidently is not difficult. Conversely, public speaking can be mastered through understanding the fundamentals of persuasion and with regular practice.

Experience is often the best teacher. When we first began 'pitching,' many of the participants, including myself, spoke with trepidation and sweaty palms. Words tumbled from my lips as my heart raced with nervousness. However, to my surprise, I was able to speak with greater conviction after just three short days of practice, and this was similarly true for the rest of my group. With a safe and supportive environment to practice among peers, I believe this boosted our confidence in public speaking, as we were able to share our most intimate thoughts aloud without fear of being judged. Seeing the growth in each of us gave me a feeling of immense pride and hope. If this was the result of three days of practice and constructive criticism, one could only imagine how much we could achieve with extended training and practice.

Another opportunity to speak up came in the "Elevator Pitch" workshop, led by Ms. Jaye Buchbinder from Stanford University and Mr. Faton Limani from the Harvard Kennedy School. In their workshop, participants were taught two key tactics to deliver a persuasive speech within 30 to 90 seconds. The first tactic, "Story Spin," introduced Professor Marshall Ganz's story framework, which opens with a protagonist facing a challenge, follows with the choices they make in response to the challenge, and concludes with lessons or values that result from those choices. The second tactic, the "Pixar Pitch," takes its cue from the animation studio, telling a story with the familiar opening of "Once upon a time," followed by "Every day," "One day," "Because of that," and eventually closing with "Until finally ..." As an exercise, delegates were invited to tell a story about themselves using either of these tactics. Though exposing our vulnerable side was frightening, I realized that sharing personal stories is also an opportunity to unload burdens. This may well have been the case both for the delegate who shared his elevator pitch for a new job, and for the one who talked about his plans for expansion with a potential buyer.

While the importance of speaking up was impressed upon us throughout the program, we were also reminded to differentiate between speaking up for the sake of getting attention and speaking up to convey a message. As leaders, it is critical that we speak up against any wrongdoing. Mr. Limani shared his personal experience of being caught at the crossroads between speaking up on an unjust issue and remaining silent. After choosing the former, he was ostracized by his colleagues. Yet, Mr. Limani confessed that he had never been more proud of himself, as he was able to stay true to his values.

"Write The Other Party's Victory Speech"

In his workshop "The Practice of Negotiation," Mr. Hungsoo S. Kim shared that negotiation skills are crucial for aspiring and current leaders, as we are constantly in the position of making transactions. It is human nature to want to win. However, if we choose a victory that benefits everyone—or, in negotiation terms, a victory that creates a "bigger pie"—we will be able to build a solid relationship in the long run with the other party. This is why it is important to begin negotiations by writing the other party's victory speech; a good negotiation is not when you have secured a good deal for yourself but when both parties believe they have attained the best possible deal.

While negotiating a win-win situation may seem simple on paper, challenges abounded when we attempted to put "give and take" into practice. My first challenge came in trying to understand the concepts of the "Best Alternative to a Negotiated Agreement" (BATNA) and the "Zone Of Possible Agreements" (ZOPA). As we practiced and debriefed after every case study, it became clearer that BATNAs could be understood as our reservation price—how much we are willing to yield to secure a beneficial outcome. ZOPA is best explained as the space between the negotiators' reservation point. Most of the time, there is room for people to negotiate and come to an agreement. However, in instances where our BATNAs are not mutually agreeable, the best outcome may be to walk away. As leaders, we must figure out how to enlarge the common ground while lessening the opposing interests so that everyone can have a "bigger pie."

The second challenge in negotiation is learning how to gain the trust of the other party, not only to achieve a good deal but also to secure a long-term relationship. This lesson was best exemplified by the third and final case study, in which the CEO of an oil company must "maximize the commercial value of, and profits from, the oil resources for the benefit of the people and the country." By the end of the exercise, there were clear winners all around the room, demonstrating that many delegates had taken the mandate to heart. However, as Mr. Kim broke down what had just transpired, we saw that for one CEO to achieve substantial profits, other CEOs had to suffer massive losses. Moreover, the collective profit or "pie" had actually become smaller. In contrast, although groups that had arranged for all the CEOs to "win," attained lower individual profit in comparison to the frontrunners, their collective pie was significantly larger.

This exercise showed that short-term gains might actually lead to long-term losses. In a capitalist society, it is unlikely that we will always be able to get rich at the expense of others, as we may one day be excluded from the negotiation table by parties we have taken advantage of in the past. For long-term gains, mutual trust is important. If one member breaks that trust, not only will other parties become wary of negotiating with him, but they may also become suspicious of every other party's true intentions, which could lead to long-term losses for everyone. This was evident in one of the groups in which one member chose to break the trust. After that, the other members became apprehensive of his promises and deemed him "untrustworthy," causing his reputation to suffer.

If we aspire to gain mutual trust as leaders, we should always seek to create value for the betterment of the community and to begin negotiations with the intention that everyone wins. Yet, how are we to know the needs of the other party? This is the third challenge in negotiation. As Mr. Kim explained, information asymmetry is present in every negotiation. While we may know our own constraints and the value we place on the task at hand, we cannot presume that the other party thinks the same way nor do we know what his alternatives are. To balance the negotiation and move towards a win-win situation, Mr. Kim brought up two words to remember—active listening.

In negotiation, active listening means going beyond just understanding and making assumptions about what has been said. Instead, we should take the discussion deeper by anticipating the interests of the other side. When we listen, we should strive to understand their BATNAs and how we can achieve ZOPA. As in Stephen Covey's *7 Habits of Highly Effective People,* active listening connotes listening with the intention to understand instead of to respond. Asking a lot of probing questions is one way we can achieve a better understanding of the other party's reservations, another is research. When we ask probing questions, we are able to make concessions gradually and come to a creative agreement. The other party operates in and learn about the challenges they face.

All too often, leaders struggle to gain consensus. Mr. Malaty-Uhr's lesson on extrinsic and intrinsic motivators proved useful during the negotiation exercise, arming me with the knowledge of people's motivations, which include their desire to fulfill their psychosocial needs —to be independent, to belong, to gain competency, or to attain comprehensive knowledge. Indeed, to practice good leadership, we must have consideration for the individual and attend to each person involved in a given issue, be it as a mentor or coach. When we understand what motivates people, and when we are considerate of what the other party needs, not only do we become more effective negotiators, we also become better leaders.

"Leadership Can Be Lonely"

The third lesson I gleaned from the ALE program is that leadership is not something we can accomplish alone. In many instances, leadership seems lonely. To anchor ourselves to the values we believe in, Mr. Limani emphasized the importance of building a support system of allies, confidants, and mentors. Besides providing assistance, a workplace ally may also provide the comfort of friendship. This is important, considering that most of us spend up to two-thirds of our waking hours at work. During trying times, allies can be relied upon to support our cause and give us the strength to soldier on. Camaraderie at the workplace also sustains a common sense of purpose and keeps us more engaged, motivated, and happy.

Mr. Limani conceded that it can be challenging to identify our true allies, as they may be supportive of one cause but disagreeable when the issue shifts. This is where confidants can play a role. Mr. Limani explained that a confidant should be someone who is not from the same company; it would be difficult to share grievances with an immediate superior or with someone who reports to us, since either party might be implicated in one form or another. They might also accidentally tell others about our issues, which would lead to dissatisfactory outcomes. In effect, the best confidants are those who cannot benefit or be disadvantaged by the choices we make.

For the majority of people, family members and close friends are natural confidants, as they already play the role of people we can rely on, gripe to about difficulties, and receive counsel from. Often, personal relationships shape the values of a leader, sometimes such relationships may even reinforce the leader's values. In Mr. Limani's case, when he asked his confidant if he should stop fighting against an unjust cause, his confidant told him to stay strong and not give in. This gave him the courage to persist in protesting the corruption at his workplace.

While confidants are important as sounding boards, they may not be in a position to help us develop our careers or have the experience to guide us to become better leaders. Therefore, the third type of person that aspiring leaders should cultivate a relationship with is a mentor, someone who can offer solid advice and a fresh point of view in order to help the leaders face their daily challenges or moments of ambiguity and turbulence. Though mentors may not be decision makers, they are in many instances the voice of sanity in times of doubt, a fact attested by many of the Fellows in different workshops.

Fully convinced of the importance of having a mentor, I asked Mr.

Kim about the qualities of a suitable mentor. He told me that a mentor should be someone willing to listen, and whose goals were aligned with my own. He emphasized that one person can have many mentors, depending on our needs. A work mentor is often a necessity for young aspiring leaders, but, as both parties grow, the mentorship may or may not continue. This is why it is good to have multiple work mentors—some to inspire and motivate us over the course of our career, others to provide necessary feedback when we are feeling lost or demotivated at the workplace.

"Everyone Is Doing the Best They Can With the Resources They Have"

When I told my friends and colleagues that I was attending a leadership program, many were curious about what lessons would be imparted, as they believed leadership was not something that needed to be learned, instead, they thought it should come naturally with positions of power. This is both dangerous and arrogant. As aspiring leaders, we should never allow ourselves to fall into the trap of thinking that there is no need for training or feedback. Far from it, good leaders recognize that learning never stops. Moreover, learning should be threefold—incorporating the learning of new skills and knowledge, unlearning of bad habits and beliefs, and relearning of best practices.

By the end of the ALE program, I learned that good leaders should proactively speak up, be considerate of others, and have the humility to take counsel from others. But above these qualities which we can all adopt to become better leaders, good character remains fundamental. Abraham Lincoln once said: "Character is like a tree, and reputation its shadow. The shadow is what we think it is, and the tree is the real thing." Without good character, speaking up may be seen as being manipulative, our consideration of others misconstrued as a lack of independent will, and seeking advice from others might be perceived as weak leadership and a failure to take responsibility. In other words, without good character, true leadership is impossible. Certainly, very few of us are willing to follow leaders who lack morals; and even fewer are willing to respect leaders we do not trust. So how do we avoid being misunderstood? What constitutes good character?

From the lessons I learned, I would say that good character boils down to having integrity and showing empathy. Integrity dictates that we conduct ourselves honestly, ethically, and honorably, regardless of the consequences. Integrity also means that our words are consistent with our actions, our values, and our principles. Above all, integrity means doing the right thing for the right reasons, even if no one is looking. Empathy is equally important as it gives us insight into what others are feeling or thinking; we become more thoughtful as we place ourselves in the other party's shoes. As Mr. Malaty-Uhr explained, we can be empathetic in our day-to-day interactions and relationships by remembering that "everyone is doing the best they can with the resources they have."

For example, many of us take for granted that our superiors should be mindful of our needs and wants, and should take pains to create a workplace environment free from politicking and unnecessary distractions. However, with empathy, we can think from the superior's perspective; is he giving me more work because he wants to add to my workload or because he trusts me? By the same token, when we think from the perspectives of our subordinates, we become conscious that they too will appreciate being told the reasons behind our actions, so that they can achieve a sense of purpose and an understanding of the importance of the task at hand.

In a media-saturated world dominated by celebrities and influential orators, society is likely to continue celebrating "natural born leaders." However, this should not stop us from taking on leadership roles if we believe we can make a positive impact on the lives of others, nor should we be fearful or hesitant when leadership roles are conferred on us. The workshops showed that leadership is something we can all learn, whether by developing persuasive speaking skills, empathy toward others or simply being humble enough to ask for help. In short, everyone has the potential to be a good leader. But in picking up the mantle of leadership, we should never compromise our character or feel pressured to give up our principles. After all, no position of leadership is worth obtaining if it requires us to abandon our awareness of the privilege it affords us in the world, whether in business or otherwise. We should also aspire to do good and leave the world better than it was yesterday; for without a sense of responsibility toward humanity, we would have failed in fulfilling the most basic tenet of good leadership.

Part 2

•

Case Method Teaching: A Way Forward for Effective Pedagogy

| Chapter 3 |

Journey to the World of Case Method of Teaching:
From Analysis to Synthesis

Dr. Cordelia Mason

●●●

Embarking on a Five-Day Intellectual Journey

In July 2016, I enrolled in the "Ethics, Power, and Decision Making" course, organized by CALI under its ALE program, to learn about Harvard's way of cultivating talents through the "case method of teaching and learning," as well as training on leadership.

As a Research Fellow by profession, with part of my duty being to write cases, I was keen to get firsthand experience of attending a class taught by faculty members from Harvard. I looked forward to immersing myself in the workshop, which promised to be experiential in its approach. I browsed the reading materials that had been sent earlier, underlining concepts and mind-mapping the key points. The night before the first class, I arranged the materials neatly in a file and made sure my colored pens were in my pencil case before calling it a day.

My colleague, Dilla, a learning and development manager in an insurance company, had also arrived, and the next morning we chatted, sharing our hopes for a fruitful training. Spending five days away from the office was quite unusual for us; most courses are conducted over two days at the most. After downing some sandwiches with a cup of tea, we proceeded to the lecture hall. I chose a corner seat in the middle section of the hall and looked around to see if there was anyone I knew besides Dilla. Spotting three of my colleagues in the front row, I waved to them, winking. They smiled.

There were close to eighty people in the hall, comprising participants, faculty members, and staff, all there to witness the opening ceremony. Noise permeated the space as excited participants chose where to sit. When everyone had settled, Mr. Hungsoo S. Kim, the President of CALI and Dr. Elizabeth Lee, the Center's Global Advisory Council member, graced the welcoming ceremony with their informative and inspiring speeches. Mr. Kim shared his concerns about the approach to education in Korea—which is exam-oriented, resulting in rote learning being dominant—and also about leadership in Asia. He lamented the lack of effective, capable, and ethical leaders in the region. Being action-oriented, however, he has capitalized on his intellectual capability and social network to share his experience of learning at Harvard with others, as a way for him to give back to society. His experience of learning in an education environment totally different from Korea's motivated him to become an ambassador of the "knowing, doing, and being" learning framework. Dr. Lee emphasized the value of developing interaction skills, as well as self-learning and cross-learning. An interesting insight that she shared was the power of being prepared: she believes that fortune favors the prepared mind. She was pleased to see the cheerful faces of the participants and wished us all an eventful learning experience.

Mr. Kim then introduced the Teaching Fellows—Mr. John Lim, Ms. Lisa Lee, Mr. Panche Kralev, and Mr. Randy Tarnowski—who would be our guides throughout the week. They each briefly shared with us their experiences of studying at Harvard and said that they hoped to apply what they had learned. Investment analyst turned educationist, Chinese American Ms. Lee, was well armed to take the educational sector by storm. Having founded the Harvard Graduate School of Education's Progressive Education Network (PEN), she was eager to facilitate youth development. For our program, she would facilitate the Personal Leadership track, the workshop I had chosen. Innovation and entrepreneurship were the two areas that Mr. Kralev was most passionate about. Having served in both private and public organizations in the Republic of Macedonia—he was the former Minister of Education and Science, as well an advisor to the Prime Minister—Mr. Kralev would guide participants on how to create shared values in pursuing entrepreneurial ventures. Mr. Tarnowski, also a recent graduate of the Harvard Graduate School of Education and former director at the Fulbright Commission in Korea, was to lead a workshop in Leadership Communication: The Art and Practice of Persuasion.

Finally, our attention was directed to the two professors, Professor Kenneth Winston and Professor Mathias Risse. They had come all the way from the Boston to be with us for a week. Professor Kenneth Winston, a retired lecturer of Ethics at the Ash Center for Democratic Governance and Innovation, is part of the Harvard Kennedy School (HKS) while Professor Mathias Risse is a Professor of Philosophy and Public Policy, also at the HKS.

After the introductions, I could feel the high energy in the air. The participants were clearly excited to embark on their intellectual journey.

The First Encounter

The first leg of the journey was Plenary 1. I felt prepared, since I had read thoroughly the assigned readings and cases. Professor Winston began his first session by giving a short overview of the case method. He described a student putting him or herself in the shoes of the protagonist or key decision maker in the case, then muddling through the very same challenge that the protagonist faced to find a solution. Professor Winston continued his lecture by quoting Spiderman: "With great power comes great responsibility."

He emphasized the need for leaders to have compassion and integrity. A true leader stands alone, with the courage to make difficult decisions and the compassion to listen to the views of others. In a case, the protagonist is a leader (all stories must have a hero) and thus his role is to go from purpose to action. The case method is designed to elicit questions surrounding a problem. The questions Professor Winston raised to get us going were: What is the problem? Why does the problem arise? What do we need to come to a resolution of the problem? What arguments can we use to think about it?

After seeing how our classes would be moderated and listening to these two gentlemen from the HKS, who have spent long years teaching ethics and decision making using the case method, my take was as follows. The case method is about developing skills of analysis by using a story, or a set of stories. It is about making decisions. It is not about giving answers, nor about providing sets of rules. What is crucial is the students' engagement with the case. The case method teaches students how to analyze complex ethical or business situations. The process can be demanding because it puts a lot of responsibility on the student, and it can be frustrating because often students simply want to know the answer. Rather than giving easy solutions, the case method encourages students to talk to each other about possibilities. The nagging question becomes, "Do you have the skills and competence to deal with the problem?" The idea is to learn how to deal with other people's problems so that you can then deal with your own. The assumptions you use are important. Though every classroom using the case method is different, the framework is not a free-flowing discussion, but rather a focused conversation about a directed question.

All in all, the overview on case method that we received was helpful for me as it confirmed from the horse's mouth my basic understanding of the teaching and learning philosophy behind the method.

Case discussion began after the overview. Our first engagement began with the "Spaulding vs. Zimmerman" case. It is a relatively short case, loaded with issues to deliberate—a case about how withholding medical information can affect the outcome of a claim, with negative consequences for the patient. As the class warmed up and each participant became increasingly engaged with the topic, opinions and ideas were thrown around the room. Most of the students could identify with the case, especially the lawyers and insurance agents among us, but also the rest, who, like people in many parts of the world, have had some dealings with medical insurance claims. We were put in the shoes of doctors, lawyers, insurance agents, plaintiffs, defendants, and family members as we agreed and disagreed, dissented and compromised, rationalized and took emotional stands on the issues. The case was, after all, about professional ethics, and therefore it had the power to rouse strong feelings in us, especially those who had been long in their profession. The participants discussed the role of ethics in professional domains, centering on codes of ethics versus common decency, and about ethical versus moral standards.

As I internalized the ideas ping-ponging across the room, I searched deep inside me for the values that I would need to make decisions on this case. Did each of the professionals depicted in the case—the family physician, Dr. Hannah, the neurologist, the lawyers, and the insurance agent—do the right thing? What are our professional duties and responsibilities, and how should we shoulder them in our working lives? What does our ethical compass look like? These questions crept into my mind as I gazed left and right, listening to the conversations taking place in Professor Winston's first class. Two major lessons that I took away from the discussion were (1) What is the right thing do to when there is a conflict between your personal and professional values? and (2) What are the consequences of a decision on the decision maker?

After a quick stop in the form of a tea break, we convened again for the next part of our journey. This time we took a trip to Siem Reap, Cambodia, as we discussed the case of Anne, a journalist, the main protagonist of "The Woman in the Corridor." Anne arrived at a regional hospital and met a woman in the corridor—brain-damaged, with no one to care for her. As we talked about the case, we delved into Anne's soul, as she discovered the meaning of humanity through her obsession with providing reasonable care for the woman in the corridor. Many questions came to mind. What should Anne do in a place where she is inundated with people who are in dire need of help? How can she strike a balance? How can she mobilize the resources to continue with her work? Does she need to draw a line, and if so, where should it be drawn? While we empathized with Anne's desperation to help the woman in the corridor, we also understood the constraints faced by the characters who were unable to help, for they had challenges of their own. Such was life for them—their normative environment, a concept which was to dominate our train of thoughts during our five-day intellectual and experiential trip.

At a personal level, I had strong feelings about the case. Having been brought up in a family of givers, I could identify with Anne. I felt the heaviness of not being able to help someone get decent treatment; of not having the resources to care beyond empathy; and of knowing that advanced medical technology and care are available only to the select few who can afford it. A high quality of life comes with a price tag. It is not for everyone. For the majority of people, a high quality of life has to be defined in many other ways. Was a smile meaningful for the woman in the corridor, a bath, a sarong to cover her up? She was, after all, brain-damaged. Or was the smile, the bath, and the sarong more meaningful to Anne, to the class participants, to me? What is this thing we call humanity? Does humanity mean the same thing to everyone?

Because of my deep interest in social economics, this case was interesting as well as meaningful to me. Having lived in different countries and cultures, I have formed the opinion that one's normative environment is a powerful tool. The session transported me back to the early '80s, when I was a student in California. I recollected the Economics classes I had taken, especially "Economic Development in Third-World Countries," which I had studied under Professor Dennis Flynn. The only difference was that we had focused in that class on South America, while this case was set in Cambodia, much closer to home and also a country I have visited for short weekend breaks. Discussing Anne's case, I relearned that one's normative environment provides the context of agency, which is defined by norms, values of different sorts, and assignments of authority. In assessing a normative environment, some questions must be asked: Who are the relevant actors? What are they obligated or permitted to do in light of their personal commitments, relationships, or roles? Who has what kind of authority?

I also learned about the distinctions between personal obligation and professional obligations, the obligation of citizenship, and the obligation inherent in being a human being. I became convinced that the normative environment must be taken seriously because decisions are made within the domain of our values and norms, which we have developed over time and are validated by the environment we operate in. The nomenclature of the normative environment is a guide for our behavior, giving us the authority to act the way we do; it is something to fall back on. I thought about how I had become accustomed to relying on my normative environment to make decisions at work. Although there were many occasions when I had questioned the status quo and made decisions that were surprising, even to myself, in general it had been easier to adapt to the existing norms. "Have I foregone some common decency in doing so?" I asked myself, as past events at work displayed themselves in my mind.

Why is it so hard to decide what constitutes common decency? How can we improve our ability to weigh what is right and what is wrong? How do we decide how to act and how to do what is right? How does the normative environment affect our decisions and our views of right and wrong?

Through the case of "The Woman in the Corridor," we learned about the theory of human compassion to help others. From what I understood from the discussion, it seems that empathy is so powerful that it can compel us to go beyond what the normative environment requires. In this case, the Cambodians, like Anne, did empathize with the brain-damaged woman but lacked the resources to go beyond their norms and to show sympathetic pity and concern for the sufferings or misfortunes of others—a feeling that Professor Risse described as "a more distanced kindness and concern for others, a double-edged sword." At this stage, Professor Risse introduced the concept of utilitarianism, which urges people to act in a way that brings about the maximal amount of net happiness compared to other available actions—in other words, it espouses the notion of the greater good.

I could certainly understand this. As the youngest of seven siblings, when I was a child, I was always the "sweet little girl," whom everyone treated with loving care. I reciprocated by bringing joy and happiness to people around me. I became good at singing and storytelling. I always fulfilled requests to sing or tell stories. This upbringing became both a blessing and a burden for me in my professional life. On the one hand, in many of the leadership roles I held, I was comfortable applying the "servant" leadership style, always willing to put the happiness of others before mine. It was easy for me because it was what I was used to. On the other hand, the value with which I had been endowed as a child has made it difficult for me to perform the control function expected of a leader. Often I have been told by "bolder" people in the office that I am weak, afraid to do what a "normal" leader would do. I do not know if that really was the case; rather, in evaluating a situation, I have always considered using my head, my heart, and my soul. Being humane is one of my core values, and I always hope to bring maximal happiness to all. I value harmony and fairness. In dealing with others, this requires a high level of tact, sometimes stressing me out as I deal with a spectrum of personalities, many of whom are less concerned about the common good. Professor Risse's explanation of utilitarianism made me think about my behavior as a leader. What does it mean to be a moral agent? What is my take on this? How strong is my moral compass?

Thinking about some decisions that I regretted, because they had made a few people think I was weak, I started questioning whether I had been a good moral agent in those instances. Professor Risse said that moral agency is not primarily about relationships but about bringing about a certain state of affairs. Was I right in fighting to prioritize kindness, empathy, justice, and harmony, instead of acting by the book and being punitive? To what extent was I wrong to forego certain parts of protocol that were difficult to amend in a highly centralized organization? Was I overindulging in the use of discretion?

My reflections went deeper as the discussions intensified. During lunch, my colleague, Dilla and I talked about the last statement written on the board: "Compassion without wisdom will not be successful. Empathy is a good gut reaction, but we need to bring wisdom in." We both chuckled as we debated whether we were any wiser than the time when we had first worked together, almost two decades ago.

Having parted ways in our careers, we had been exposed to different normative environments. It felt good to share our thoughts, although our hearts were still heavy from the analysis of the "The Woman in the Corridor," which was daunting for both of us in many ways. We both agreed that it was a good case. The first leg of the journey had been a beneficial one for us.

The Debrief: Taking a Step Back

During our intellectual journey, we made stopovers in the form of small study group sessions, to pause and revisit what we had learned so far. These sessions allowed us to take a step back and reflect before we made any more steps forward.

There is no doubt that the plenary sessions struck the deepest chords of my learning needs. I was very much inspired by Professor Winston and Professor Risse's engagement with the class. At first, I thought they were just professors who had come to impose their normative environment on us, as a sort of one-way information flow. However, as we sat through their sessions, my resistance to learning melted bit by bit. My frozen mind softened, and I became ready to be filled with wisdom and insights. By the third day, I was already contemplating quitting my job to enroll at the HKS. Given my current normative environment, I knew this was just wishful thinking, as the lifelong learner in me rose to the surface! Can our normative environment be changed? Can the ethical standards surrounding our normative environment change? I choose to think they can. In the five days of our intellectual journey, I explored ten different cases, each bringing with it a contrasting idea about ethics. Although I have taken many classes on ethics and embedded ethics in my own lectures on various areas of management, learning from, and with Professor Winston and Professor Risse via the case method was very refreshing. It felt as though the files on ethics stored in my brain all these years were reformatted, as if I could now use new apps to think about ethics and apply ethics in my decision making.

In our journey, we boarded two "trains of thought" about ethics. On the first train, our captain was Professor Winston. On the second train, the captain was Professor Risse. The two professors took us through two different routes. Captain Winston's route focused on what I consider to be "micro" or "internal" topics: the cases we discussed with him were about protagonists who wrote about ethical challenges that had affected them personally. Captain Risse's route was more "macro" in nature: his cases focused on how one's decisions affect the bigger population. Let's get on board now.

Key Takeaways from Captain Winston's Train

Captain Winston guided us through five topics on ethics: (1) A Framework for Professional Ethics; (2) Personal Convictions & Public Decision Making; (3) The Ethics of Obedience & Dissent; (4) Ethics in a Non-Ideal World; and (5) The Ethics of Exercising Power. To fuel our thoughts about these issues, he provided us with seven cases: (1) Spaulding v. Zimmerman, which has been touched upon earlier in this essay; (2) A Gift of Life; (3) Hunter v. Norman; (4) The Tax Collector; (5) The Cancer Patient; (6) The Prison Master's Dilemma; and (7) Relying on Hard and Soft Sells, India Pushes Sterilization.

Professor Winston stated that ethics is really very simple, with only three possibilities (see Figure 1):

Ethical Conflict
Right versus Wrong Right versus Right Wrong versus Wrong

He taught us about a technique of analysis called "stepping on the balcony," which offers a way to look at issues from the outside in. To get a neutral view, one simply needs to disengage oneself from the problem. At first I could not relate the three possibilities to each of the cases, but by the third day it became apparent that "Spaulding v. Zimmerman" was clearly a right v. wrong ethical conflict, while the "Prison Master's Dilemma" case, in which a government official succumbs to unethical conduct when pressured by an unethical politician, was wrong v. wrong.

The "Gift of Life" case was interesting to me because the protagonist is a doctor from Singapore, very near to where I live. With many doctors in my family—my paternal grandfather was a doctor, my eldest brother is a pathologist, two sisters are dentists, both married to medical doctors, and one of them has five children, who are all doctors—I can vividly imagine the many dilemmas facing the medical fraternity on a daily basis. I recalled an anesthetist friend of mine, who told me about why he always waits as long as he can before applying anesthetics to his patients. One day, he had just finished the procedure on an aged patient when a lady in her forties walked into the patient's room and wept. She hadn't spoken to her mother for a long time, due to a misunderstanding. She lived overseas, and upon hearing of her mother's operation, which had only a 50-50 chance of success, she flew back immediately. However, her flight was delayed, and when she reached the hospital, her mother had just been given the anesthetics. The operation was unsuccessful, and her mother never woke up again. It was heart-wrenching for my friend to see this woman next to her mother's deathbed. Since then, he has never treated the procedure as simply a time-based activity to be rushed in the name of efficiency.

"The Gift of Life" is about a professional ethical standard at odds with the doctor's personal ethical code. It describes the tension between his belief in saving life at all costs and his professional ethical obligation to cater to the request of a patient, the hospital's client. The main insight that I gathered from the case was that a single code of ethics cannot settle all ethical questions. The case demonstrated the need for us to learn about finding common ground in three spheres: the personal sphere, the professional sphere, and the public sphere.

On reflection, I believe that this case is about how we can stay true both to our profession and to our calling to serve the greater good. We need to see beyond the shortsightedness of our clients and to prioritize values. As we cannot give life to a person, it must be preserved at all costs. And as a doctor, the protagonist shows the core of his own values when he makes the decision to save the baby. To draw an analogy: as a teacher, my task is to facilitate learning. Therefore, I must be conscious of the approach I take when solving problems relating to learning, to ensure that I lead students toward the advancement of their knowledge instead of the retardation of their intellect.

The cases of Hunter, Khalil, Ahmed, and Poorva all revolved around what to do when facing conflicts with the accepted practices of their workplaces. Hunter's case was a conflict regarding timeliness and misinformation; the case of Ahmed, the tax collector, was about dealing with political patronage; and Poorva's case was about dealing with a cancer patient's request for treatment. I identified well with Poorva because I usually prefer to make the logical decision, especially if the choice is between life and death, but I would make sure to justify my actions in writing. I am a strong proponent of using discretion when the situation calls for it and, later, to recommend changes that fit the changing needs of the stakeholders. I am brave enough to make an unorthodox decision if my conviction in making it is strong. I will choose to be answerable. That is why I identified most with Poorva.

I also found the case of Khalil, the Prison Master, interesting, as I considered how a change in his view "from the balcony" affected his decisions and career path, and how his ethical values changed across time. His experience applies to many others around the globe; when you seek a different vantage point for looking into yourself, the learning opportunity to know your own ethical standards is massive.

>Overall, the ride on Captain Winston's train enabled us:
>(1) To see moral competence as a set of virtues:
>   I. The virtue of civility;
>   II. The virtue of prudence;
>   III. The virtue of balance; and
>   IV. The virtue of respect.
>(2) To appreciate proficiency in institutional design; and
>(3) To be able to reflect (a double layer of reflection) on how to think about ethics. To realize that there are dif-

ferent ways of thinking, that maybe my way of thinking is wrong, and that maybe others are wrong too.

Is there anything I can do to continue to learn and grow? I am sure there is. Riding on Captain Winston's train has confirmed that learning is continual, at least for me.

Key Takeaways from Captain Risse's Train

As said earlier, Captain Risse's train was running on bigger tracks. The cases focused on issues that are familiar internationally, namely (1) The Woman in the Corridor; (2) German Constitutional Court: Authorization to Shoot Down Aircraft in the Aviation Security Act; (3) George W. Bush on Iraq's Nuclear Weapons; (4) Hero or Traitor? Edward Snowden and the NSA Spying Program; and (5) Aung San Suu Kyi, Seizing the Moment: Soaring Hopes and Tough Constraints in Myanmar's Unfolding Democracy.

I enjoyed reading and discussing all these cases. "The Woman in the Corridor" has been discussed earlier. The second case, on the German Aviation Act, was about taking human life seriously. I was reminded of the MH17 tragedy, in which the pilot was my husband's schoolmate. People must be given the right to be consulted when the matter is a human life—in other words, human beings are endowed with dignity and inalienable rights. The right to life is supreme, and therefore the state has the duty to protect life. Also emphasized was Kant's idea of never treating anybody as a means to an end. George W. Bush's case was about lying and deceiving, and we learned about intentional deception, lying, and negligent deception, as well as concealment. Two types of thinkers about moral agency, the consequentialist and the deontologist, were brought on to the scene. The former thinks of moral agency simply as a means of bringing about good consequences, while the latter thinks that certain actions are inherently problematic, regardless of consequences. We were asked to ponder, for example, the question of why lying is such a bad thing.

Snowden's case was a hit. Divided into two groups, we had to decide whether Snowden was a hero or a traitor. My initial reaction was to join the group that thought he was a hero. However, as all five of my colleagues were already in that group, I decided to join the group that thought he was a traitor. I sat on the fence initially, but after the group discussion I tilted toward the opinion that Snowden is a traitor. Too much damage has been done to privacy of information, and, given the threat of terrorism, I decided that we do not need another Snowden. What he exposed about the American government was not news to me. It is an open secret. His actions caused more harm than good, in my opinion. At that point, I knew I was leaning toward the utilitarianism school of thought. The program had certainly achieved its aims—I was learning about ethics effectively.

In contrast to the Snowden case, the case on Suu Kyi got only lackluster attention from the participants. Professor Risse was concerned. Why were the participants disinterested? I had been relatively quiet in class, as I strongly believe that taking turns is an important aspect of the case method and that no one should dominate the discussion. Mind you, it was hard to suppress my frequent urge to share an opinion, but I was steadfast in my resolve to allow others to talk and to be a better listener. Nevertheless, as comments were few during this session, I shared my own views of the case. Suu Kyi was prominent in her battle for democracy, and in my formative years, I was filled with admiration for her struggle. I waited for the time when she would prove herself an effective leader, like other daughters of prominent heroes around Asia who were instrumental in our fight against colonization: Indira Gandhi, Sheikh Hasina, Benazir Bhutto, and Megawati Sukarnoputri. But the long wait for Suu Kyi's success and her rather cold views on the Rohingya migrant issue left me disappointed. The ethics of her leadership could be analyzed using the concept of normative environment, and we also looked at the Machiavellian theory. We discussed adaptive leadership and examined leadership as a moral operation. The idea that every situation requires a different leader also surfaced.

Our journey with Captain Risse ended with a hypothesis, which states that immoral leadership—leadership that fails to empower people to deal with challenges in a lasting way—will often fail. The lesson for me was to stay clear of immoral leadership in my own work as a leader as much as I can. I must constantly refer to my compass of ethics at work and at home.

Conclusion

The five-day program about ethics, power, and decision making provided an invaluable experience. Analyzing the cases gave me the opportunity to develop and enhance my teaching skills. The experiential learning approach was highly effective. I certainly gained insights on how to teach cases more effectively through this five-day intellectual journey.

The course enabled me to reflect upon how I have fared in my teaching career especially in my quest to promote learning through the problem-based approach in which case studies are used extensively especially in management classes. It also brought back memories of how I enjoyed learning using cases during my undergraduate studies in California. In a sense, although that was thirty years ago, the excitement of reading cases and analyzing them was reignited during the course. I am thankful to have joined this program and hope to share what I learned with others.

| Chapter 4 |
Seek First to Understand

Dr. Hendry Ng

● ● ●

"Let every person be quick to hear, slow to speak, slow to anger." James 1:19

I surprised myself by agreeing to what was stated in the email dated July 29, 2016: "We would like to nominate you to attend the "Case Method" program, organized by CALI." My other appointments were promptly re-scheduled. In ticking my choice of the workshop, "Case Method Teaching: A Way Forward for Effective Pedagogy" in the application form, I naively gave "refresher of case methods" as an a priori reason to join the program from August 8-12, 2016. I was reassured that my son Rufus, who had participated in a similar program hosted by CALI about two years before, gave a good report of it.

During the five-day workshop, as I arrived each day for breakfast at 7:30 a.m., my body and mind were sluggish, due to my late-night reading of cases for the next day's session. Each day, I swung from an initial reluctance to effervescent engagement with my fellow participants and facilitators, before winding down blissfully after the last session in the afternoon. Whether this rigorous schedule was character-building or not, it was certainly far from my normal routine.

What I Learned

During the five-day program, Professor Mathias Risse and Professor Kenneth Winston of the Harvard Kennedy School were the key facilitators of ten plenary sessions. Case studies on "Personal Leadership: Ethics, Power, and Decision Making" were used throughout the sessions. These cases offer narratives of how their protagonists' personal moral values collide with their professional codes of ethics, causing conflicts between them and the normative environments of their communities.

Both professors reminded us that we do not live in a vacuum but in milieus that dictate us what to value, and what actions and decisions are appropriate. They adeptly guided our discussions on why people behave the way they do, and eventually I became thoroughly annoyed by people's subservience to societal norms.

Often, outsiders are the ones to challenge the status quo. In the case of "The Woman in the Corridor," the outsider is Anne, the UN-hired Chief Technical Officer at a training institute for Cambodian journalists. But a local person may also become an activist, as seen in the case of "Hero or Traitor: Edward Snowden and NSA Spying Program." In the case of "The Prison Master's Dilemma," the protagonist is captivated by egalitarian practices while studying abroad in western Europe and consequently attempts to introduce changes to his workplace, the prison. Some people prefer to overcome challenging issues in a subtle manner, as in the case of "The Tax Collector," while others prefer to work within the system, as in the case of "Aung San Suu Kyi, Seizing the Moment: Soaring Hopes and Tough Constraints in Myanmar's Unfolding Democracy." In the case of "Relying on Hard and Soft Sells, India pushes Sterilization," different people promote different methods for solving a national issue of overpopulation. While some confront problems head-on, others prefer to leave their environment to evade further conflicts, as in the cases of "The Tax Collector" and "A Gift of Life"—though, as Professor Winston pointed out, the decision of Dr. Henry to quit his job assignment in "A Gift of Life" was not an act of civility.[1]

Sensing that some participants would arrive at a quandary, Professor Risse introduced another entity—"others," those people distinct from ourselves and the people around us. These "others" often provide the alternative yet noteworthy views, which are helpful in unraveling ethical issues. In the workshop, he included René Descartes and Niccolo Machiavelli.

Descartes defines knowledge in terms of doubt, because he understands doubt as the contrast of certainty. Doubt and certainly are inversely related—when certainty increases, doubt decreases, and vice versa. Knowledge, in Descartes' definition, is based in complete certainty, without any traces of doubt.[2] He states further that true

---

[1] Civility is the hard work of staying present even among those with whom we have deep-rooted and fierce disagreements. Politically, it means negotiating interpersonal power so that everyone's voice is heard and nobody's is ignored.

[2] Descartes refers to this as an *indubitability*, or inability to undermine one's

knowledge is a conviction based on a reason so strong that it can never be shaken by any stronger reason.

Machiavellianism today is often used as an unflattering term to characterize unscrupulous people. Machiavelli believed that public and private morality should be understood as two different things in order for a ruler to rule effectively. In *The Prince*, he suggests that the social benefits of stability and security can be achieved in the face of moral corruption. For that reason, a ruler must not be overly concerned with reputation and must be willing to act immorally when it will serve his ends to do so.

Both Descartes and Machiavelli offer ways of tackling the exigencies of making ethical decisions. Machiavelli condones the strategic exercise of brute force and deceit, including "categorically killing," a competition to head off any chance of a challenge. More abstractly, Descartes exhorts us, when in doubt, to seek certainty through knowledge. So, I pondered upon Aung San Suu Kyi's deafening silence on the plight of the Rohingyas in Burma that could be seen as somewhat Machiavellian. However, the Cartesian (of Descartes) view has urged me to seek an explanation for her inaction. In her interview by an Indian news channel in Nov 2012, she explained that she had not spoken on behalf of Rohingya Muslims because she wanted to promote reconciliation between the Buddhist and Muslim communities. Despite NLP's victory in the national elections in 2015, the military still retains 25 percent of the seats in parliament and controls several key ministries under a constitution that bars Suu Kyi from becoming president. I think she knows civility is necessary for

---

conviction.

democracy. Her present concerns are apparently straightforward—reconciling the Burmese and the restive minorities, and providing reassurances to the prowling military.

My Purpose in Writing

Upon returning to the tyranny of work, I ruminated on what I had learned about the virtue of civility and Cartesian's view of "seeking first to understand." I cogitated whether the maxim was applicable to my present work as the Director of a Transnational Higher Education (TNHE) program in a private institute of higher education.

I have written this narrative as a way of describing the persons, agencies, and dynamics involved in administering a Masters in Business Administration (MBA) program in a twinning arrangement with a foreign university. It seeks to unravel the epistemological[3] puzzle of transnational higher education, teasing out the various elements that contribute to its practice, including the role of quality assurance agencies (e.g. the Malaysian Qualifications Agency or MQA) in creating program standards, and the shifting expectations and demands of the students (e.g. employability, entrepreneurship). With these considerations in mind, I then make an argument for why a strong brand ecosystem, by continually introducing innovations, will engage new students and other stakeholders, thus staying relevant in a changing world.

---

3 Narrowly defined, epistemology is the study or a theory of the nature and grounds of knowledge, especially with reference to its limits and validity.

Transnational Higher Education

Educational traditions are changing. Local students who would once have traveled overseas to pursue international qualifications are now studying foreign university degrees at local institutes of higher education (IHE).

This area of the international education market is referred to as transnational higher education (TNHE). In Malaysia, the TNHE landscape is mostly populated by private IHEs. The most common are in-country partner arrangements, including the franchising, twinning, or validating of degree programs at local IHEs by institutions in countries like Australia and the U.K. Degrees are also sometimes granted across borders by international branch campuses of foreign universities.

The prevalence of TNHE programs has come about because of social and cultural norms, economic necessity, and political convenience. People leverage education to escape the cycle of poverty and scale the social ladder. And the Malaysian government allows TNHE courses onshore as a safety valve, to defuse the social tension precipitated by limited public university placements and overseas scholarships.

TNHE comes in different shapes and sizes. Essentially, it is the exportation of higher education programs, delivering degrees across borders to remote learners in numerous and growing forms. TNHE is becoming highly commoditized, and, as a result, IHEs need to innovate and think outside the limits of their traditions. When basic facilities and resources, such as classrooms, lecturers, and libraries, are expected by everyone, forward-looking IHEs must differentiate themselves with innovative services, including student learning experiences, blended learning, multimedia case studies, and other out-of-the-box delivery and assessment methods.

The Author

I graduated with a Bachelor's degree in Computer Science. After that, I worked for eight years in a supporting role as an Information System Manager before deciding to come out of the closet and pursue a Master's program. I earned an MBA in IT management and then completed a Doctorate in Business Administration (DBA). In 1991, I had my first experience of transnational higher education. As the coordinator of a U.K. undergraduate program at a local college, I worked with an American professor to co-develop the first-year curriculum of a twinning program.

My present employer is Gordon College, a reputable private institute of higher education in Malaysia's Klang Valley that was started by a business corporation in 1987.[4] My position, for the past seven years, has been the Director of the MBA Program. Since 2004, Gordon College has offered an MBA program of a top-ranked Australian university. When it was launched, there were less than fifteen MBA programs in the country. Today, there are more than two hundred, in both public and private IHEs.

In my first interview for the job, I responded to all the questions with much enthusiasm. I spoke about the importance of committed teaching staff, memorable student experiences, and an efficient office

---

[4] I've changed the name of the college to protect its privacy.

in a successful academic program. After my second interview, I got the job.

My predecessor gave me a short briefing on my responsibilities, and then I was left to learn the ropes from the administrative assistants. A newly appointed Deputy Vice Chancellor of Postgraduate Programs visited my office once but otherwise left me alone. Looking back, I realize that my institute was enthralled by its ambition of becoming a private university.

Although I had held similar position in other colleges, it took me several months to navigate the new college—its academic direction of top management, its academic staff, and its partner university. Because I was in charge of a twinning program,[5] there was not much I could change in the syllabi of its courses. However, the partner university was prepared to adjust the delivery and assessment methods to suit the local market. With that in mind, I went about attempting to differentiate our MBA from the offerings of other colleges, first focusing on the students' expectations from an MBA. Our intakes improved over the first three years.

A year ago, our partner university announced a new set of entry requirements for the MBA program. I was alarmed by the change because the new requirements would affect future intakes. Based on their entry qualifications, at least 25 percent of our current students

---

5 Many choose the twinning route because it is financially viable compared to spending all three years overseas. Students on twinning programs can study one year locally and two years abroad, or two years locally and one year abroad. Many reputable universities in Australia, Canada, New Zealand, the U.K., and the U.S. offer twinning programs. Alternatively, students can complete a 3+0 foreign Bachelor's program, in which foreign study programs are conducted by private IHEs in Malaysia.

would not be admitted. I voiced my concerns during the Partnership Advisory Board meeting that year. Sure enough, the number of current active students plummeted. So I earnestly asked the obvious:

- What is transnational higher education?
- Should education be a business?
- How then should one lead an academic institution?
- Who are the MBA students?
- Why is the theory-practice integration approach to MBA delivery so touted?
- With myriad MBA programs in the market, how should our MBA be branded?
- What will the next game-changer be in the crowded MBA market?

After several months of soul-searching, I have come to a new understanding of our environment. There are glimpses of order in the apparently chaotic tumbling. From my research into the insights of MBA students (what they want), the pedagogy of MBA programs (what to teach them), workplaces in a volatile, uncertain, complex, and ambiguous world (how to facilitate theory-practice integration), and the evolution of transnational higher education (anywhere-anytime learning), the model of a sustainable MBA program is slowly taking shape in my mind.

Regulating the Quality of Education

A recent directive from the MQA states that a minimal cumulative grade point average (CGPA) of 3.00 must be attained by all MBA students in order for them to be eligible for graduation. This has caused immediate non-conformance by many foreign programs that do not use the CGPA grading system.

The presence of quality assurance agencies strongly indicates a lack of trust in IHEs to self-regulate effectively. The principles and guidelines underpinning the foreign partnerships of U.K. institutions are overseen by the Quality Assurance Agency. Similarly, the MQA regulates Malaysian education, and the Tertiary Education Quality System Agency (TEQSA) of Australia covers offshore partnerships as well. The regulatory role of these quality assurance agencies seems justifiable and necessary for TNHE. On the other hand, the agencies sometimes create extreme pressure for local institutes, asking them to conform to MQA standards that are incompatible with the policies of their partners, the foreign universities.

It is an ongoing debate whether an educational institution should be managed as a business entity. While it might seem that my role as a program director is informed by principles independent of the business objectives of Gordon College, increasingly it seems that the reverse is true. A program director's allegiance belongs, first and foremost, to the owner of the institute. This type of dependence leads directors to consider very carefully what actions would be right for business, but not necessarily whether such actions are ethically right for academic purposes. Thus, the question of who should be responsible for regulating academic standards becomes increasingly complicated.

The MBA Students

Swee Lan, a native of Malaysia, went over to London as an exchange student and then landed an internship. The same firm then hired her as a full-time accounting staff, and the last time I heard she was still gainfully employed.

Daniel, an Iranian student, had earned a professional accounting qualification. He was given an advanced standing of six subjects so that he could complete the remainder of his courses in a shorter study period. His intention, he told me, was to emigrate to Australia. Aiming for a transfer after passing the first two courses of his program, he began to enquire about the transfer procedure. The partner university in Melbourne gave him the approval. But the Australian Immigration Department rejected his plea. He was deeply disappointed, and I feel that I may have been at fault for not informing him about his slim chances of getting a student visa, due to the lack of diplomatic ties between Iran and Australia.

Unlike Daniel, Devan, another student, was given a student visa to complete his MBA study in Melbourne. After completing his studies at the University of South Australia, however, he spent a year looking for a permanent job and then could not afford to remain in the country any longer. His meager wages from the odd jobs he could find were not enough to pay his expenses.

Understanding the students and their aspirations is critical to achieving high student satisfaction. Bad student experience means bad business. I therefore took great care to ascertain what students want. Several surveys about our MBA offerings have provided new insights. First, the students seek a flexible format that will allow them to pursue an MBA in the way that suits them best. Clearly, there is a growing trend of blended learning, possibly using methods outside the regular study routines of the classroom. Second, students are increasingly "glocal students"—local students with global aspirations, who want to enroll in globally administered programs in a local setting. These students display far more sophisticated and nuanced characteristics than I had first expected. Third, most of the students will not leave their jobs. As "career alumni," they are focusing on their own professional development and seeking a high-quality program that will lead to career enhancement with their current employers. Fourth, the students value the professional networks gained from their MBA studies.

In short, the students enrolling in our programs are preoccupied with their employability and career advancement. A higher quality of education and the hope of improving their career prospects have always been among the most important factors for them. Moreover, though they often can't afford the costs of living and studying overseas, they are eager for any experience of living abroad. It thus dawned on me that perhaps a compromise could be reached—by having them spend their final semester at a partner-university campus.

The Pedagogy of an MBA Program

When John came into my office, he was quite lost. He had failed in his recent business, which he had founded in partnership with two of his fellow graduates after their undergraduate years. Without any work experience, they had ventured into starting a restaurant. John had persuaded his father to loan him RM350,000, which was the amount expected from each partner. The restaurant had gone well until, in its second year, the partnership went sour and the business folded. At the end of two meetings on separate weekends, we agreed that for John, the MBA program would be a time to reflect on his failed business and to seek professional renewal and regeneration. John met with me regularly throughout his program. In his last semester, he was hired as a General Manager of a TGI Friday's outlet. What got him the job was his experience with a failed business—ironically, his knowledge of failure was his most valuable asset, one that his new employer could appreciate. But not all MBA students are like John.

In seeking to understand students' aspirations, an equally in-depth understanding of the business world is crucial for curriculum development. An MBA program must integrate the theories and concepts learned in class with real-world practices in workplaces. Interviews with distraught students revealed to me that most lack competence in theory/practice integration—there is a gaping disconnect in their minds between what they know in theory and how to apply it in practice. But if an MBA program is an incubator of high-performing managers, there must be some way to help the students remedy this disconnect. I urged our facilitators to rethink their pedagogical approach to each lesson. If they first define the theory, they should then cite workplace examples to demonstrate the theory in action. Inversely, if a lesson starts with an observable phenomenon in a workplace, the facilitator should then guide his students to look for an underpinning theory.

In both of these methods, Harvard's case study system is useful to facilitators and students. However, not all cases are useful[6]. For the students to appreciate the relevance of the case, the class discussion must evolve to a high enough level of abstraction where ideas are theorized. As a learning tool, case discussion leads to specific learning outcomes. For that, the case teacher would prepare a teaching note that contains a case summary, teaching objectives, study questions, class discussion, reflections, and suggested reading list. Most MBA students are technically competent in their own fields. And they may not be familiar with issues outside their own knowledge domains. During the session, the case teacher may first ensure the students are clear about the context, players and issues, or he may just let the students find out for themselves. Cases which are conflict provoking are likely to induce good discussion, especially for the sake of the less participative students. In this way, the peer learning takes place in class. For case study as an assessment, marks are allocated for class participation and post-discussion reports by the students.

Cases are useful for decision forcing because problem solving skills are so much touted. If MBA students are being prepared to overcome volatile, uncertain, complex, and ambiguous business situations, they ought to be familiar with all the possible ways of solving such problems. Often at workplaces, senior managers function as the drivers of the organizational machine. An organizational goal is interpreted and broken down into several tasks that must be accomplished. The manager must delegate these tasks to several layers of management, and, the people below them, at the operational level, actually carry out the

---

6 Robyn, D. 1986 "What makes a good case" *Case Program*, Kennedy School of Government. A good teaching case serves a teaching purpose (pedagogic utility), and is conflict provoking, decision forcing, generalizability to a larger class of managerial or analytic problems, and of appropriate brevity.

tasks. Managers who exploit "command-and-control" tactics often rely on rewards and punishments to get things done through their subordinates, assuming that those subordinates will do what they are told.

Cases should be of appropriate brevity. This is because too many facts can be distractive. But businesses are not simple organizations. I pondered upon the view of Murray Gell-Mann that successful business enterprises are complex adaptive systems[7]—"jaguars" that can identify irregularities in their environments and interact with entities both within and outside the borders of their environments. Organizations, on the other hand, represent what they have experienced in models for future use—predicting and acting on similar problems. But when they are fixated on developing a model for each type of problem, they often carelessly ignore changes to the initial conditions[8]. So, it is crucial to strike the right balance between simplifying a case study to make it manageable and retaining enough of its complexity to make it pedagogically relevant.

---

7   Gell-Mann, M. 1995, *The Quark and the Jaguar: Adventures in the Simple and the Complex*, New York: Henry Holt & Co LLC. An adaptive system is able to learn from a changing environment and act accordingly. Murray Gell-Mann differentiates between the quark (the basic building-block of all matter), which cannot learn, and the jaguar, which can. Business enterprises ought to be jaguars.
8   Lorenz, E. 1993 *The Essence of Chaos*, University of Washington Press. Chaos theory states that any solution is inevitably sensitive to the initial conditions and to the assumptions used in deriving the solution.

A Brand Ecosystem

MBA programs are highly commoditized. Like all IHEs, the MBA program of Gordon College is a business that offers a particular brand.[9] Based on Michael E. Porter's view,[10] the business activities of designing, producing, delivering, communicating, and supporting products must lead to an increase in substantive value for customers. Similarly, Kotler and Keller[11] opine that customer value is created and renewed through interactions between the stakeholders (customers, company, and collaborators) and value-based activities (value exploration, value creation, and value delivery). From these view, I extrapolated that student experiences are critical to building a strong brand. The experiences include both academic and extracurricular experiences—student life, sports, community activities, etc. The stakeholders include the employers, professional bodies, and alumni, who all contribute to the student experiences.

So, Gordon College ought to listen to the students' needs and wants in order to create a brand ecosystem,[12] in which all aspects of the experience conform to overarching guidelines, focusing on stimulating interactions between stakeholders and the students. It is a "participative branding" approach of engaging all stakeholders, earn-

---

9 A brand is a product, service, or concept that is publicly distinguished from other products, services, or concepts so that it can be easily communicated and marketed.

10 Robben, X. 2015 Michael Porter's value chain, 50MINUTES.com.

11 Kotler, P. & Keller, *K.L Marketing Management*, 15th edn. Pearson India Education Services.

12 A brand ecosystem is an organic model in which an institute's management listens to the conversations happening around it, energizing those conversations with interesting content and experiences.

ing both their attention and their participation through experiences. It informs Gordon College about the desired value propositions of a high quality brand. To do so, Gordon College ought to operationalize, measure, and test the effects of each of its brand elements. Student experiences must be measurable in terms of the perceived quality of the services and facilities, including the library, industrial links, student life, sports, recreations, and brand loyalty.

Conclusion

The maxim "seek first to understand" is the most valuable thing I learned in the five-day CALI program. In facing any future conundrum, I will not act on my first instincts but will instead seek clarity in understanding the people and circumstances around me, as well as soliciting alternative views from "others."

Civility is the hard work of staying relevant as an IHE. There is so much that I still need to learn about transnational higher education. It is a dynamic system, highly sensitive to changing conditions. Small differences—for instance, a change in educational policy in a host country or in a partner university—yield widely diverging outcomes, rendering long-term planning unreliable. In addition, the new, highly digitized environment of education is disrupting traditional classroom teaching. As a result, our teaching and learning methods must be continually updated to suit new demands. And the curriculum must be regularly revised to reflect the real-world predicaments faced by students in their workplaces.

Student experience is the central element of Gordon College's brand. The institution's brand ecosystem focuses on bringing together input from all the key stakeholders in order to provide the most nuanced information as we craft meaningful brand strategies. In this way, the MBA brand of Gordon College keeps re-inventing itself, acting on what is happening in the community so it can quickly react and offer new student experiences. The richer the student experiences, the stronger the brand of the MBA program. As the Director of the MBA Program, I too must keep re-engineering my role, so that I can deliver the best possible product to both my employer and my students.

Part 3

Personal Leadership: Ethics, Power, and Decision Making

| Chapter 5 |

The Ethics of Deciding between People and Rules

Elma Berisha

● ● ●

One challenge I have recently become aware of is the need to strike a balance between upholding an ethical principle and not alienating people by doing so. A corollary challenge is not to be marginalized for taking a stand, something that recently happened to me when I uncompromisingly upheld an ethical principle and, as a result, ended up losing my connection with the people involved. Such decision making processes are agonizing, and yet the hallmark of ethical behavior is to bring harmony to yourself and to the people around you.

It has always been my baseline assumption that all ethical principles and rules are aimed at ensuring the good of the people. As long as this is true, there is no reason for people to come into conflict with those ethical principles. At the same time, I have often wondered about my own position: Am I too rigidly principled or rule-bound? Or, on the contrary, am I too people-oriented? Which one of these tendencies is stronger in me? I can easily be convinced to go the extra mile for either of these motivations, on the one hand being empathetic to people and on the other hand, upholding abstract principles. Thus, on certain occasions, I not only end up being torn in opposite directions, I find myself strongly inclined to go the extra mile in both directions at once!

The Workshop

I revisited my questions about ethics, rules, relationships, and cultural norms when I enrolled in the "Ethics, Power, and Decision Making" program, organized by CALI, under its ALE program. This program ran concurrently with the "Case Method Teaching: A Way Forward for Effective Pedagogy" workshop. And, interestingly, it was the case method of teaching that made the whole difference for me. The method placed the program participants in the role of decision makers to confront some of the greatest ethical dilemmas of our times. Teaching by the case method involved no prior scripts and no ready-made answers. In the words of Professor Kenneth Winston, "It is not the teacher's function to be an oracle of some moral truth, let alone to elaborate general theories."[1] Each case offered a unique problem and context, likely causes of the problem, decision making protagonists facing specific dilemmas, and potential solutions, each with a rationale and consequences. Classes unfolded with much student engagement and lively discussions about real-world cases and problem solving scenarios. The method thus elicited a great deal of self-awareness and reflections on multiple levels, beyond the usual scope

---

1   Kenneth Winston, "Teaching with Cases," in *Teaching Criminal Justice Ethics: Strategic Issues*, edited by John Kleinig and Margaret Leland Smith (1996).

of classroom teaching.

After a week of plenary sessions, interactive workshops, and energetic debates, in which we deconstructed ethical conundrums one by one, I noticed a pattern in myself, a tendency to favor people in need over rules. Ultimately, this discovery challenged my self-perception that I was too rule-bound. Did the empathetic, people-oriented side of me finally tip the balance in its favor? Over the years, have I experienced a change of heart in regard to rules and principles? In this essay, I have contemplated these questions, discussing some personal experiences in an attempt to expand my understanding of these concepts.

Bound by the Word

The interplay between upholding ethical principles, complying with rules, and abiding by cultural norms is sometimes too fluid to discern clearly. In common parlance, however, these terms are often used interchangeably: principles, values, norms, rules. The thin line separating these concepts is apparent even in the *Oxford Dictionary*'s definitions: a "rule" is "one of a set of explicit or understood regulations or principles governing conduct or procedure within a particular area of activity."[2] By contrast, a principle to me seems more like the philosophy behind an act or activity. Cultural norms are mostly social standards, expectations of how we ought to behave, whereas a rule provides an explicit regulation, which must be followed, it would seem, regardless of one's ethical values. In other words, following the rule could be simply procedural. Another way to define ethics, as op-

---

2   https://en.oxforddictionaries.com/definition/rule.

posed to rules, is through the absence of an explicit penalty system. Ethics are self-imposed moral principles, while laws and rules, if broken, will incur penalties. In this essay, I refer to rules as a common method of underpinning norms for our explicit and implicit social arrangements.

When I was younger, I did not differentiate between principles and rules, and so this whole dialectic was perplexing for me. As a child, when I was given a task either at school or at home, an instruction to do something or not to do something, it served as the final word: no matter what came my way, I would never break the rule or deviate from the instruction. In hindsight, this was not so much a blind following of a specific instruction as an unconscious upholding of an underpinning principle: "I will fulfill my commitments no matter what," or "I never break a promise." In my case, breaching a rule was not an issue of rule compliance but rather an issue of principled promise-keeping. And while abiding by this principle, I risked going against other principles. Being bound by my word sometimes meant disobeying a second authority who gave me a second instruction contrary to the first. My principle thus led me into puzzling situations.

Trust as a Blueprint of Ethics

I became aware of the importance of trust on the first day of the ALE program. At first it seemed unrelated to our ethical debates, but I soon realized that people have to trust and rely on each other for any social interaction to happen at all. Rules by themselves are not sufficient to ensure ethical behavior. Indeed, trust is indispensable in ethics. It's the cornerstone, the tool by which any notion of ethics is made possible. Even with trust, however, since humans are known to be unpredictable, norms and rules are necessary to facilitate the social interactions and fortify the trust involved.

I became aware of this necessity while working in our family business of video rentals. I was about ten when I first began to work at our home-based outlet. In the beginning, I would fill in for my father for a few hours when he had an engagement downtown. Later, when the summer holidays began, I started working full time. At that time there were no satellite channels or streaming options available like Netflix. Moreover, given our political situation, in which our national Kosovar TV headquarters was usurped and blocked for years by the occupying Serbian police—who were dubbed the most militarized police in Europe at that time—video clubs like my family's played a key role in distributing popularly produced content in our native language. In the collapsing communist legacy of a centralized economy and media, such local private production was crucial for the survival of our national spirit.

In our video club, we had a set of rules that I followed dutifully. For instance, customers needed to have a personal ID to rent videos from our store. The rules themselves were quite simple, but the people and scenarios I encountered were often complex. Denying a graceful auntie was a hard thing to do. She might have forgotten her ID or not had cash on hand when she came to our outlet. Perhaps she was too tired from a day's work to go home and come back. I often felt compelled to compromise. She might say, "Oh, I am Erza's mum and your aunt's friend! Remember last summer in Germia?" and I would remember. Or she might say, "Child, don't you trust me?!"

and I would feel rude not giving in. Or she might say, "Come on, it's ridiculous," and I would feel embarrassed. It was a small town, after all. I found that automatically distrusting people was an impossible thing to do. Upholding the rules did not mean that I distrusted the people involved. It was simply procedural. As a result, I circumvented the rules when acquaintances came by. The rules were helpful, but for me the process of trusting people and evaluating customers never became mechanically utilitarian or scientific. I didn't do it by following rules; my process was more intuitive. And I felt that there was an ethical burden on me: how was I to judge people and decide if they were trustworthy or not? How could I tell someone, "Sorry, I cannot allow you to rent the film because you do not seem trustworthy to me"? That was too much of a challenge for an overly polite child. And crafting a fictional excuse for not renting videos to such customers felt unethical too. Thus, the burden at all times lay with me.

If, as often happened, the customers complied with the collection deadlines and payments, I gained another inch in my trust of other humans. These first experiences in public sphere were the building blocks of my positive convictions about human nature. I tended to generalize, assuming that goodness in human nature was a given, while the contradictory instances I classified as exceptions to the norm.

People Come First

By the time we had discussed a few case studies in the week-long ALE program, it became apparent to me that I prioritized people over rules. Thus, in the "Hunter versus Norman" case, which we debated in the "Ethics of Obedience and Dissent" session, I advocated accommodating Senator Hunter's paperwork appeal, regardless of whether the glitch of "misinformation" from the assistant of the clerk's office had taken place or not. When Hunter called the office to ask if he has to appear in person to file the petition, the assistant affirmed it unaware that the requirement to appear in person was only for filing the consent form. Hunter was running for the Democratic primary and then the general election, and he was required by law to secure signatures for a nominating petition and to file those signature by a specific deadline. The deadline for the consent form was at a later date. He ended up being three minutes late in submitting the required petitions in person, and Jane Norman, the administrative officer in charge, refused to accept his petition papers because of this delay. Thus Hunter lost the right to appear in the upcoming ballot. He took the issue to court, and the Federal Court of Appeals ruled in his favor, allowing him to proceed to the ballot and thus prioritizing the benefit of the general public. If Hunter had not been allowed to proceed, the general public would have been deprived of a petitioned candidate. It seemed to me that this was a case of people in need versus operational rules.

I could also relate to the dilemma narrated in the "Women in the Corridor" case, which we discussed in the "Our Common Humanity" sessions. The protagonist, Anne, was a trainer of professional journalists working on a temporary, non-profit basis in Cambodia. She found herself going out of her way to help people whom she barely knew. At that time Cambodia was experiencing political instability, and massive protests in the streets led to a turmoil of explosions and people getting injured. Anne had to track down her journalist co-workers in Cambodia's poorly maintained hospitals and make sure they received the necessary care. But she couldn't restrain herself from helping other people along the way. At times, she financed strangers' healthcare out of her own pocket. The case vividly illustrated the difference between seeing the victims of conflict in person or only on TV. The barrier of distance was not there to excuse Anne from extending her aid to those in dire need, though there were also no professional obligation for her to engage in these acts of kindness. Her personal ethical standards reached beyond her professional ethical standards. Neither her normative environment (her journalist network) nor Cambodia's cultural norms dictated her ethical duties to Anne, but her own inner voice told her that this was a case of people in need being more important than her surrounding cultural and professional norms.

Most people think of ethics as a series of rules to be upheld. Experience, moreover, has shown that some rules produce the greatest happiness for the greatest number of people.[3] Thus, in ideal terms, ethical rules (and motivations) and utilitarian calculations (and consequences) should be in tune. However, the case of "The German Constitutional Court," which we discussed in the "Taking Each Person Seriously" session, clearly illustrated the tension between the ethics of rules, namely deontology, and the ethics of utility or utilitarianism. This was a case in which the German constitutional court overturned the Aviation Security Act, which authorized the armed forces to shoot down a hijacked aircraft, if and only if the aircraft was intended to be used as a weapon threatening human lives. The rationale of the

---

[3] Dave Robinson & Chris Garratt, *Introducing Ethics* (2013).

Aviation Act was that more human lives would be saved if the aircraft were shot down. Utilitarian might argue that human rights should be subject to the promotion of the greatest good within a society, meaning that the individual's rights can be compromised or denied if that will yield greater benefits for society as a whole. The German Constitutional Court, however, overturned the Act, judging that it is the duty of the state to protect all human life and not to convert human beings into numbers by making utility calculations. Human rights are inalienable and universal, and that is a fundamental rule or principle. The promotion of the greatest happiness for the greatest number cannot justify the violation of any individual's welfare.[4]

As we debated this and other cases, I noticed that the more closely a case study involved individual people, the more empathic I felt toward them. The more the writer described individual people's predicaments, the more prone I was to prioritize the people over rules or utility trade-offs. In the cases in which individuals were not directly involved, or when people remained an abstract notion with no real individuals involved, I leaned toward the strict upholding of rules. In the case of "The Prison Master's Dilemma," which we discussed in the "Ethics in a Non-Ideal World" session, I opted for the middle ground in our negotiations. A corrupt minister threatened to deprive the protagonist, Khalil, of his job unless he compromised the transparency of the hiring process. Khalil refused to bend the rules and resigned. Even when the minister offered compensations, Khalil refused to be co-opted. In this case, the author did not spend much

---

[4] Andrew Heard, *The Challenges of Utilitarianism and Relativism in Human Rights: Chimeras in Sheep's Clothing?* (1997).

time portraying the individual qualified applicants who would lose out in case Khalil gave in to the minister's pressure; they were referred to simply as an abstract group. The writer spent more time describing the good work that Khalil did in reforming the system. Thus, the loss of his job seemed to me like a more immediate risk. But I wonder, had I met those applicants in person and appreciated their hard work and sacrifices, then, if I would have made the same decision as Khalil. By resigning, Khalil did not help those qualified applicants at all. Jobs went to the minister's undeserving acquaintances anyway. For Khalil, it was not a matter of choosing between rules and people in need. It was a matter of professional integrity, a matter of principles versus personal relationships, in this case his relationship with the minister.

The Ethics of Rules versus the Ethics of Principles

The case of "The Cancer Patient," which we debated in the "Ethics of Obedience and Dissent" session, provided an explicit illustration of the difference between the ethics of rules and the ethics of principles. Poorva, the protagonist, was appointed as a chief executive governmental officer in a remote district of her country. She decided to go ahead with this role despite her family's objections. It was her mission to help the remote areas affected by many social ills, and she was also in charge of supervising the public health system of the district. The healthcare facilities in the district were far from adequate. One day a poor cancer patient arrived at her door, pleading for financial support so that he could continue his journey to the specialist hospital in the capital city. The cancer patient had heard of the government's new healthcare scheme to help the citizens with their medical expenses, but he was not aware that the scheme had procedural rules and caveats. It would take time for the application process to be completed and the approvals to be received. Poorva tried to explain the matter to him, but the patient was weak, sick, and unable to return back to his remote village if his request was rejected. Poorva was in a difficult situation. She was aware that the healthcare rules had been established with the overarching objective of helping the people. On the other hand, the scheme and its rules were newly set, untested, and unsophisticated.

In this case, therefore, the ethics of rules, which are transactional in nature, came into conflict with the ethics of principle, which are transformational in nature. The ethics of rules require compliance and maintenance, as opposed to the ethics of principles, which encourage growth and adaptability. Poorva decided to bend the rules and help the patient seek a cure. She undercut the imperfect bureaucratic regulation in order to help an individual patient, and she did so at her own risk. For Poorva, the rule was only a tentative embodiment of an ethical principle: to help people in need. For her, helping individuals felt like a moral duty, a mission, and all else, rules included, was subservient to that mission. So, in this case, ethical intent mattered more than the consequences. The patient, ultimately, was not saved, but no one was hurt in the process neither, except, potentially, for Poorva herself, who could have been reprimanded for breaking the rules.

The Quicksand of Changing Rules

Rules are sometimes difficult to follow. A social or cultural system of monolithic rules is confining if it does not allow room for alternatives. If a system of rules or norms is too rigid and fails to take into account the inevitable exceptions, it may come to embody an anti-life stance, for life, by nature, keeps evolving, and systems regulating the social interactions should follow suit. "Where roads are made I lose my way," says Tagore. New situations are always arising, and if the rules do not change accordingly, they represent an anti-learning approach. Their rigidity suggests a failure to learn from emerging opportunities, from challenges and risks, from immediate surrounding. Thus, ethical questions often arise not because some people do not comply with the rules but because there is a confusion about existing rules as they apply to unprecedented scenarios. The newly emerging and controversial fields of bioengineering, fintech, and geo-engineering are cases in point. On August 27, 2016, *The Economist* argued, "New technologies, from sharing economy apps to blockchain, offer routes around some of the trust deficits that stand in the way of growth. Yet, whether such solutions to problems of mistrust build on or undermine social ties is no easy question to answer."

In pre-modern times, the life-over-rule rate of change was slower and more manageable. Nowadays, this rate of change will only increase. Given the fast pace of technological developments, no rules are likely to hold for long. Our society's rules will have to be reinvented quickly—but, at the same time, it will be necessary to maintain some form of permanency and longevity over time. If it is too easy to break a rule, then that rule has no meaning; people will simply find self-serving reasons to circumvent it. The challenge is that people are unlikely to abide by a regulation today that they know will change tomorrow. They will either simply wait for it to change or rush ahead before the new rule is introduced, depending on their situations.

Therefore, norms and regulations, even if they are temporary, remain useful only if they are perceived as permanent and indispensable. That perception of stability is necessary for the "manufactured normalcy field"[5] to function. So, while globalization has helped us transcend parochialism, it also risks instituting a slippery slope of constant change, which does not fit well with our human need for predictability, familiarity, and stability.

Caution, Slippery Slope Ahead

Unlike rules and norms, principles transcend people, times, and locality. They serve as the existential fiber of any ethical system. Overarching ethical principles make rules and norms possible in the first place. Here, I allude to universal ethical principles, for instance the "golden rule," or the principle of contract fulfillment: "Do unto others as you would have them do unto you" (Matt. 7:12). This principle forces a reasonable perspective from all parties. It balances self-interest, which is natural and not necessarily bad, with other people's interests, which are equally worthy and, by the same token, not necessarily bad. A good ethical system must be a practical one, which acknowledges all perspectives and denies none.

An unethical system is one that teaches us to embrace unbalanced self-interest and plays upon the essentializing of others, a rationalization that falsely appeases our ethical concerns and moral obligations. In the "fundamental attribution error,"[6] we tend to attribute our own

---

5 Ziauddin Sardar, *Welcome to Post Normal Times* (2011), ziauddinsardar.com.
6 Mark Sherman, *Why We Don't Give Each Other a Break* (2014), https://www.psychologytoday.com.

faults to inessential circumstances that have nothing to do with our fundamental values, while we attribute others' faults to their inherent traits and values, ignoring their surrounding circumstances. This shuns away our ethical obligation to help others and hurts our moral growth. As Kant argued, ethical systems are predicated on a conscious struggle against actions that come to us naturally.[7] Being ethical entails regulating what we want to do, disciplining our primary inclinations, and channeling our impulses into a wider vision that extends beyond self-interest. Obviously what comes naturally to us is self-interested. Dismissing our moral obligations and blaming others is often the easiest thing to do and accords with our self-interest, but it is not ethical behavior.[8]

A few years ago, in one of the Smithsonian's museums in Washington, D.C., I stood in front of a statue of Rosa Parks. I had vaguely heard of her before, but her story, inscribed on the base of the statue, struck me deeply as an exemplary case of rule-challenging. While the segregation of "colored" people in public spheres was still in a full swing in the city of Montgomery, Alabama, Rosa refused, at the risk of her life, to give up her seat to a white passenger in a public bus. The civil rights movement triggered by this act of defiance quickly gathered momentum, and Montgomery soon had no choice but to lift the law requiring segregation on public buses. Rosa Parks received many accolades during her lifetime. She had defied a rule in obedience to a higher principle, the principle of civil egalitarianism.

Nevertheless, the slippery slope here is steep, and unfortunately

---

7   Dave Robinson & Chris Garratt, *Introducing Ethics* (2013).
8   Ibid.

the opposite could also hold true. Some of the most terrible things in history have happened with a similar rationalization of principle over rule, principle over people. Unethical actions are too often carried out in the name of a high principle, and frequently great numbers of people have been brainwashed into believing such rationalizations. In a name of a principle or value or ideal, people have been killed, imprisoned, and dismissed as valuable participants in society. It was this realization of the potential of abuse inherent in all principles and values, as much as in rules and regulations that tipped the balance in me of empathy over rules. I am still as people-oriented as I was before, but I am no longer as rigidly principled or rule-bound as I used to be. Learning by the case method made this realization possible.

The Roots of the Matter

Yet, one may never be able to figure it out once and for all. Ethics is a complicated subject matter in theory let alone in culturally-embedded crossroads of life. In ethics, if the inter-relationship between people, rules and principles is elusive, the underpinning cultural processes that often work unconsciously, make it even more. Thus, just like rules and principles can be rationalized to take advantage of people, so can the people themselves be rationalized to take advantage of other people. In the name of ideals, principles, values, and rules, unethical conducts can happen. In the name of 'people in need' too, unethical conduct can happen. In the name of anything good, unethical conduct can happen.

The biggest loss that I incurred in my video club was when an uncle came in to rent a video and a few movies, tagging along his sick kid. With gestures mimicking pain and care, the father said the kid was just discharged from the hospital. Besides the few bandages on both his limbs, the kid was obviously pale. In this case, I did follow the rules by textbook. But, had I been more cautious, I should not have rented the video, given that the customer was not from our town. This was the single fact which I ignored distracted by the conversations with the sick kid and his enthusiasm for the titles in offer. The father abused the kid. The customer never came back to return the products nor pick up his ID, which I had diligently kept. Rules were not enough. None had the time to chase him out of the town as it made no economic sense. With the dysfunctioning state of affairs overall in our occupied country, it did not make sense to file a police report either.

However, given the absence of rule of law and its reinforcement by legitimate state authorities, in hindsight, these types of misconducts were miraculously infrequent. Perhaps in a social condition of besiegement and oppression, people get to solidarize with each other, learn to not let each other down. Trust increases and mutual help substitutes the missing legal infrastructures. Perhaps these are the ideal times when the principled bond of community reigns over explicit rules which are not reinforceable anyway. The penalty for breaking a rule is absent. Thus, community makes sure to establish a more reassuring trust structure. In normal times, one breaks the rule, one gets penalized for that specific case. In emergency times, which I spent most of my childhood in, one breaks the community trust, one loses everything. These ethical principles were the overarching pinnacle of any social interactions that must have influenced my attitudes of principles over rules and people over rules! It might also have been an underpinning cultural implication in my hometown that principle is to die-hard for. In tough times of Balkan wars, that's what has kept our nation historically alive. On the other hand, the petty rules were often set up by our interim occupiers, be it Serbs, Ottomans, Communists, and so on. Therefore, the attention to rules was likely lower. The rules were less respectful in a way, compared to ethical principles. I look back what were the stories that our family cherished. Was it about national heroes 'who bent the rules to help the people in need?' Almost all the time. In the language of my culture, a Rosa Park may sound very familiar.

Navigating the Way Ahead

The worst kind of leadership deems people incapable of making their own choices; it assumes that people must be forced to comply with their society's rules. This position leads inevitably to over-regulation, and in the long run it will backfire. Good leaders, by contrast, not only figure out the best principles and values to nourish, they set up adaptable rules and regulations; encourage people's compliance via innate motivation rather than top-down imposition; and, most importantly, pay attention to people's feedback. Open systems have proven to be the most resilient, as they grow organically, and the people grow symbiotically with them. Because they are allowed both interaction and participation, people come to respect open systems of social regulation. They assume a degree of authorship and ownership of their society, and thus their ethical principles can align with the society's rules and norms.

| Chapter 6 |

First Impressions—Lasting Impact:
A Hard Lesson in Humility

Yasmin M. Handrich

●●●

First, allow me to say that I have never saved a life, nor ever been the victim of any crime or severe misfortune. All in all, I have lived a very fortunate, some might even say a sheltered life. This story goes back to first impressions and snap judgments, something we all experience consciously or subconsciously. They are an evolutionary necessity for effective recognition and survival. The extent to which we either hold onto them or else adjust our behavior according to subsequent information is what sets apart "open" people from narrow-minded "stereotypists." This story is about the power that first impressions have to influence events long after they have been formed. It is also about how we, as well-educated, mature, and ethical beings, ought to be careful in managing their effects on our decision making. It demonstrates the importance of pushing ourselves to rise above our first impressions.

With this essay, I will be divulging a part of me to you. A part that

I rather wish never happened, an episode of my life that I reflect on often and ask myself 'what if'? While this episode of my career happened quite some time ago, it stuck with me because looking back, I can ever so clearly see all the tiny interconnected pieces that led to its culmination. How after some initial struggles, I allowed myself and my pride to rise before the inevitable fall. It made me wish that I had more of an ability to rise above those petty first impressions, admit wrongdoings more easily, learn from them, and rise above the emotional baggage they create, to live a freer, more carefree, more compassionate life.

The expression "sticking out like a sore thumb" might have been invented for me. Fitting in was never really my thing. I am a twenty-seven-year-old German girl who has spent the past eleven years living in Malaysia. I followed my parents here initially: my father worked in the petrochemical industry. My family has since departed, but I stayed behind to continue the life I had built here, one complete with an apartment, a long-term partner, and a dog. Being a "Westerner" in a developing country often comes with high superficial value. I've lost count of the times I have been asked incredulously, "Why would a German want to live here, in Malaysia?!" by stunned locals. For me, the answer was simple and yet complex. When you feel like you don't fit in where you come from, anywhere can be your home. Moreover, I soon started enjoying the automatic high regard that I received from locals and the stereotypes that labeled me as punctual, meticulous, diligent, and potentially full of high-quality ideas, before I even opened my mouth. I prided myself on my lack of a discernible accent and my "walking encyclopedia" status. The alienating feeling of being different that had smothered me as teenager in Malaysia, when any attention was both unwanted and awkward, had turned into a full-fledged craving to be someone special. Why would anyone wish to leave that feeling behind?

But along with my assumed habits of punctuality and meticulousness, came traits that conflicted with the standards of my new home. Being German, I am overly critical, pessimistic, and forthright. One might classify me as overbearing, and I am easily capable of landing myself in political or personal hot water. I struggled to reconcile these two conflicting identities, being at the same time someone chastised by her peers for overusing the word "sorry" someone who always assumes that any misfortune is somehow her fault.

This inherent conflict found expression in a fundamental, perhaps even childish desire to elicit happiness in those around me. I tried my utmost not to cause grief or be at fault, as a way of reassuring myself that I was likeable and accepted despite my overbearing nature. You might call people like me the social glue, mothers of the group, social butterflies, people connectors, etc. The role even became my first job, at a management consulting company that I joined as a recent graduate and stayed in for almost five years. A member of the social committee, the stationery queen, the office psychiatrist, the unofficial party planner—you name it, I was involved in it. And when I eventually left this identity to begin a new job, although it was something I yearned for professionally, my departure caused me a great deal of heartache.

Fortunately, I had already built a great rapport with my soon-to-be co-workers and manager, and after the administrative transition, I was excited to resume my "productivity mode" in my new job. But the two-month break that I took in between the two jobs was dearly needed. I had felt so burned out in my previous job that I made it a point during the interview process to tell my new employer that my primary reason for changing employers was my desire for a more balanced personal life. I was happy to be reassured that this would be possible in my new job, and also that the organizational culture fit my personality. But this latter comment left me wondering, typically, if I was truly qualified to hit the ground running. Was my understanding of project management what it needed to be? Was my knowledge of brand health sufficient? I appeased my worries with my favorite HR mantra: "Hire for attitude, because skills can be taught." If nothing else, the right attitude, I felt, was something I truly had.

So there I was, twenty-seven years old, embarking on my first day as a manager in a brand new company. I felt happy and proud, as my new employer was a globally recognized powerhouse in the research industry. I considered myself even luckier that my first day coincided with a department-wide, week-long training boot camp. Surely this training would allow me to gain a good understanding of the finer technical details needed for my new role, which I still feared I wasn't fully qualified for. Bright and early I made my way that morning to the company's rather remote destination, where I was happy to see a lovely breakfast spread, including a fabulous selection of tea. I prepared a concoction of chamomile tea to calm my nerves, with some honey to start my day on a sweet note. I was eager to make my mark on this new group of people. I grabbed my cup and entered the conference hall where the training would be held. It was of medium size, with a capacity for perhaps ninety to one hundred twenty people, in five rows of tables seating three people each. It was still early, so only a few of my new colleagues had already arrived. I selected a seat at the back next to two lovely-looking Chinese ladies, Conny and May,[1] who seemed to about be my age. They turned out to be local Chinese who had joined my employer as recent graduate executives and worked their way up to become senior executives within a couple of years.

I quickly discovered that first impressions can be flawed: for the remainder of the week, both my tablemates, lovely-looking though they were, seemed to try their best to be as clique-ish and stand-offish as possible. After my first carefree attempts to get to know them were greeted with terse responses, I resigned myself to asking only the most pertinent technical questions, and soon I stopped even that, after meeting their judging eyes at each response. Usually I believe in the old German adage that "As you call into the forest, so will the echo come back to you." In this situation, however, I had no idea what I had done to warrant the kind of treatment I was receiving. I comforted myself with the conclusion that I had simply made the wrong choice in seating, without being privy to the larger forces at play. Who knew what their circumstances may have been at the time, but to me being unkind to a stranger was not something easy to forgive.

For those who have seen Roger Sanchez's video for "Another Chance," I don't need to explain what happened next.[2] In the video, a cheerful young lady leaves her home holding a gigantic heart in her hands. She carries it around the city and is greeted with coldness and bewilderment at the size of her heart. As she does so, the heart

---

[1] Names have been altered to protect individual identities.
[2] https://www.youtube.com/watch?v=rdlvPe959Ck.

shrinks, until at the end of the day there is nothing but a fist-sized heart left for her to hold. And so my week continued. My actual teammates, though superficially friendly, chose to sit among themselves, leading me to stay put as well. My repeated inquiries about the team's projects were met with a profound aloofness. When I attempted to inject some fun into the day by participating in a guessing game, it went awry. All in all, I was left wondering if there were some kind of conspiracy underway to make me feel unwelcome.

At the end of the week, I left the training boot camp feeling utterly dejected. I had learned that breaking into this new social circle would be an uphill battle. And though I took the weekend to recuperate, my transition into my new role still proved to be unexpectedly rough. In the first six months, over and over again, I discovered that the hiring manager had given me the wrong expectations about what my new work-life balance would be. We used to call ourselves vampires, for we never saw the sunlight. Still, I tried to take the long hours in stride and buried myself in my work. At this point, I had all but given up hope of enjoying any social aspect of the job. In fact, the only reason why I stuck around—or so I told my concerned mother when she called to check that I was still alive—was to prove to myself that I could overcome this challenge. The proverb "When it rains it pours" seemed to have been created for my situation, but there wasn't much point in complaining over a path already chosen. The hard work and sleepless nights would be rewarded eventually, I was sure. These haven't been my expectations on that first, optimistic morning of training, but they formed my new reality.

The next four years passed in a breeze. And in a true vindication of the power of endurance, I saw blessing after blessing come my way.

First, I grew close with my department teammates. Even though we only spent time together working, not even eating lunch together—who has time for lunch?—we managed to become friends, and having even one companion was more than I had hoped for after that first week of training. Next, my original hiring manager was replaced by an amazing new director who took the role of leadership to new heights. Our team soon grew to ten people, and while others came and went, I stayed put for more than four years, making me the "dinosaur" of the team. The new director and I formed a great partnership. We developed business together, executed projects, played "good cop, bad cop," hired new teammates, and worked hard but played even harder. Although I am clearly biased, I would say that, had there been a competition for the Most Fun Team, we would have been a shoo-in. We caught a lucky break when, one to two years into my tenure, the management decided to change the office design, going from a very traditional, multi-level, ring arrangement to a single-floor, open-concept layout. The new office did more for team integration than anything I had seen to date. We were fortunate enough to witness the transformation of the past "silo" office culture into a family-like culture that everyone enjoyed and felt proud of. We may have been "slogging like slaves," but we stayed for the people, our second family.

Along with the hard work, recognition was abundant. The senior management bestowed multiple awards on me and my team, based on our stellar business growth and strong client-servicing skills. As I watched my profile become more prominent in the company, I felt happy to have re-established my previous role of mother hen, stationery queen, and all-round technical advisor. As an HR-appraised "high performer," I knew that my career was on the fast track, with plenty of prestigious opportunities in sight. It had taken some time, a lot of personal growth, and perseverance, but I had finally managed to make the new company my home. They were my second family, and I was a respected and productive member of it. Reflecting back on these times, I feel proud of the significant progress that I made during these four years of service, in large part thanks to my management, who saw the potential in me and took the time and effort to groom it. For that I was and am truly grateful.

Through the years, two major insights stood out to me. First, you can never be universally liked. Second, change, for better or worse, is inevitable. I learned the first lesson by coming to realize that Conny and May were part of a larger "cool crowd" in the office. Since I stuck to my own devices for the first six months of my tenure, I did not pay much attention to them or their clique. But I had numerous irritating interactions with members of the clique, who worked in a support function that I directly liaised with. Because of the way they conducted themselves—their immaculate manners, spotless work, universal likeability, and seeming inability to do anything poorly— the rest of us started referring to them as the "Teflon Gang": like Teflon, they seemed to be able to deflect all criticism or dirt without any effort. Annoying though they were, in time I came around to a more zen-like view of the "Teflon Gang." I gave credit where credit was due and tried to be the bigger person when others sniped at them. A few years into my tenure, during a roundtable discussion, one of the Gang members commented to our regional managing director (MD) that the company should recognize its "more quiet associates, who often seemed to be neglected in favor of their more flamboyant colleagues." I was surprised by the courage it must have taken to voice such a grievance with our senior management. I knew she was referring to me in using the word "flamboyant," but in that instant I decided, rather than taking the comment as a slight, to view it as a compliment. My decision was validated when our MD responded that, while "no one's achievement should be neglected, and the company took great trouble to recognize and foster talent, there also had to be recognition for the extra mile that "flamboyant" people cover in their efforts to integrate people, make them feel happy. Their efforts positively influence the team's motivation and in turn its work."

So I carried on my quest to develop expertise in my industry, strengthen my research skills, and forge lasting relationships with my clients. At this point, I had been given quite a lot of autonomy in my day-to-day dealings. I held a diverse portfolio of large and small accounts, counting among my clients, major local and international banks and insurance providers, as well as a local industry regulator. The regulator had developed into my favorite client account, and business was going well. We had several large and small projects running across various departments with them, won in large part due to excellent referral feedback that we had obtained from the client departments. It was a fact to be proud of, both for the team and for myself. So much for the first lesson learned.

The second insight, about the inevitability of change, was a mantra that we embraced in the company. If you felt comfortable in your role, you would be assigned stretch tasks. People had great job mobility, and my own manager changed repeatedly in the span of four years. It should not have come as a shock to me when, three years into my tenure, my manager called the team together to inform us that he would be departing in two weeks. Nevertheless, I felt betrayed: why, I thought, would he have kept this from me for so long? I also felt sad, for I knew it would be the end of a comfortable era, and I didn't know if I had it in me to adjust to yet another manager and prove myself all over again. Then another anxiety set in: what did this mean for me, for us, for the team? To whom would we be reporting?

Our new director turned out to be an amiable man called Jerry, whom we had enthusiastically adopted into our team when he first arrived. Jerry was nice, polite, and extremely witty, and he had warmed up to us immediately. Since we had no direct working relationship with him, we got to reap only the benefits of his presence in the office. These included years of research expertise, an ever-entertaining desk partner, and wild stories of cross-country escapades during lunch. To my dismay, I discovered within a few weeks of his arrival that my original hiring manager had influenced the decision of who would be hired as a main executor of one of our new projects, alongside Jerry. It was Conny, who, as part of the "Teflon Gang," had left behind a great impression with our management. To her credit, she was significantly nicer and more approachable in her new role. And I knew that, as with Jerry, we would have no direct dealings with her. I decided to try my best to welcome her back into our fold.

Now, I'm sure that the company management did not plan for this to happen; I'm sure they were simply trying their best to cope with a difficult situation. Nevertheless, after our old manager left, something happened that proved disastrous: we were told that Jerry and Conny would be merging with our team and that Jerry would become our new director. While we were lucky in one sense, having gotten to know our new boss in an informal manner beforehand, there were still tensions from the get-go. It isn't easy to fill the shoes of a manager as beloved as our departing one. Neither is it easy to transition from working with someone as a colleague to working with that same person as a boss. On Jerry's side, his already established working relationship with Conny introduced a certain amount of bias. She had been his primary point of consultation at work thus far, and so, naturally, she became his primary point of reference in his new role. I have to be honest and say that this irked me more than once; at times it even made me feel lonely, in an "us versus them" kind of way.

Months followed, in which I lamented to my friends and family about how this rearrangement had ruined the professional bliss I had become accustomed to. I constantly felt as if I were under observation, as if the new management were purposefully hunting for reasons to persecute and chastise me. I felt that Jerry was being overly critical and singling me out. This in turn made me even more defensive and stand-off-ish in my dealings with him. After several months spent trying to accommodate each other, the tension between Jerry and me came to a head during the performance appraisal of one of the associates in our team. I felt that the associate was being unfairly judged, while Jerry felt that I was being overly protective. It was a battle for control between the new and the old management. The discussion culminated in Jerry elevating his voice, clearly exasperated with my repeated attempts to argue with him on this and other matters. Suddenly I realized that I had driven a polite and calm professional to the point of saying, "Just shut up, will you." In metaphorical terms, I had lost a father figure and was unwilling to defer to my new step-dad's authority.

After this incident, Jerry and I had a private and frank discussion about the aspects of my behavior that he did not appreciate and would not tolerate, and I in turn voiced my unhappiness over being subjected to so much scrutiny. While I conceded that he was indeed my manager, I pointed out that the title alone didn't automatically mean I would accept him as my leader or give him the respect he felt he deserved. We reflected on our relationship, wondered how it had come this far, and brainstormed about what we could do to patch things up. Needless to say, the meeting was transformative. And with our mutual respect renewed and our tensions eased, I was able to regain my equilibrium and concentrate on my work.

In the "Case Method Teaching" program, I was particularly fascinated by the case of Henry, a religious man who became a doctor to help society. Despite his best efforts, he found himself in a situation in which his personal values conflicted with his professional duties: though he held strong views against abortion, he was asked to step in and conclude a "botched" abortion begun by another physician. Our workshop group intensely debated whether his personal or his professional code of ethics ought to prevail. For me, Henry's case held an uncomfortable level of personal resonance.

I had always been aware of the market research code of conduct, issued by the World Association of Opinion and Marketing Research Professionals (formerly the European Society for Opinion and Marketing Research, also known as ESOMAR). However, I had never taken the time to familiarize myself in detail with the code, as the concepts seemed like common sense to me. I conduct myself with a high degree of integrity at work, not hiding anything from my peers, my management, or my clients, and I consider myself a good, ethical, honest person. Yet, despite my high personal standards, I once came into conflict with Article 4 of the ESOMAR code, which reads as follows: "Researchers shall ensure that market research projects are designed, carried out, reported and documented accurately, transparently and objectively."[3]

This next part is hard to write because coming to terms with our personal failures is never easy. Inevitably, we look for circumstances that may excuse them. I could emphasize that I had been consistently working more than twelve hours a day, or that every weekend I had to find a balance between my personal life and a mounting backlog of work. I could say that after reporting to three different people, I was sick of proving myself over and over again, or that my mother-in-law had just succumbed to cancer and I was reeling from her loss. I could say that it was not my job to do the task in question, or that I had five other projects to look after and was simply too busy. But all of these explanations, in the end, can't hide the fact that pride and carelessness led me to my biggest professional mistake and a painful ethical dilemma.

A few months after Jerry had taken over as our director, but before our heated discussion, I had been tasked with running a very valuable, very high-profile project for one of our most prestigious clients. The account fell within my portfolio, and Jerry and I led the bidding process. I was ecstatic when the news came that we had won—especially because Jerry and our management knew that we had been included in the process only at the last minute, because of our existing client team's recommendation. The new project was a repeat study,

---

[3] https://www.esomar.org/uploads/public/knowledge-and-standards/codes-and-guidelines/ICCESOMAR Code English.pdf.

but the scope and servicing model needed a complete overhaul. I saw my chance to make my mark with it, but Jerry announced that he too wanted to be kept abreast of the project's direction, not only because of the high-profile nature of the study but also because the project was personally interesting to him. At the time, this statement seemed like an affront to my sense of autonomy. While nodding in agreement to him, I vowed internally to aim for minimal interference. This was my account, I had been handling it long before he ever came onboard, and I doubted the value add he represented. In fact, I saw it as an attempt to take credit and assert his influence on the account.

After completing the client alignment, the project set-up stage commenced. For more than six months, the allocated associate and I worked tirelessly, overhauling the questionnaire, drawing up a representative sampling frame, overseeing the fieldwork, interpreting data, establishing analysis frameworks, and writing and rewriting reports. The project took much longer than usual, as the client was attentive to even the smallest details, and we spent many hours aligning tiny decimal-point differences, finding exact terminology, and perfecting data positioning. The exercise culminated in our presentation to various high-ranking officials on the client side, and we then watched excitedly as our findings were published in the mainstream media. In the long-run our findings would serve as basis for national policy development decisions.

The client allowed us comparatively free rein in this process, as they had little to no expertise in the area, but, as per my usual style, I was fully transparent and walked them through every step of the process. This was one of the reasons that the client team appreciated us as a research partner. Our main concerns were the maintenance of a meaningful exchange with the client, the usability of the final output, and the potential for a knowledge transfer. After our dealings with the client had finally come to a close, we held internal knowledge-sharing sessions with our team in which we elaborated on the project's objective, the execution metrics, and the analysis framework. Overall we were very proud of our achievements and felt as we closed the chapter that it had been a job well done.

Or so we thought. Eight months later, on a hectic Tuesday afternoon, a chat ping popped up on my laptop screen. It was the associate who had collaborated with me on the project. She said that she was in a room with Conny, working on another project that had direct involvement from our regional managing director. They were trying to make certain claims about Malaysian consumers and were using our study as a basis, since it was recent and comprehensive. My first thought was "Why!?" I felt very bothered by her seemingly random inquiry, especially since the project had come to a close for such a long time already. Our professional relationship had never warmed, and I avoided interactions where I could at all costs. Both Conny and the associate should have known that data was proprietary and therefore could not be used in another client's project. Instead of saying this, however, I tried to understand more about the problem they were facing. I knew the associate was familiar with the study herself, so perhaps I was simply misunderstanding her query. She explained that they were trying to draw parallels on usage statistics but that the demographic profiles of respondents didn't seem to tally. Could I have a look to see if she was looking at the data in the right way? I told her that I was quite busy but that I would look at it the following day, which was a public holiday. And that was the end of our conversation for the day. But something in the back of my head started nagging at me. Was it possible that we had made a mistake? The nagging feeling wouldn't leave me, but I had bigger priorities to deal with at the time, so I put the thought on the back burner and focused on the task at hand.

That night, I didn't sleep very well. The part of me that immediately assumes I have done something wrong was in full swing. I felt sure that we had executed the study perfectly and that if I just looked at the data I would reassure myself that everything was fine. But I couldn't shake my petulant thoughts: "What were they doing in the first place, digging in my study?" The next morning, I powered up my laptop, pulled up the sampling frame of my study, and vetted it thoroughly. It looked consistent within itself, with no calculation errors. Next, I examined the data my associate had sent for comparative purposes, and I realized that indeed there was a mismatch between their respondent profile and ours. To find out why, I went to look at the sourcing of our sampling frame data, which should always be noted on the bottom of the data table. In our case, however, it was missing.

I tried to collect my thoughts. The study, at this point, had been done almost a year ago. I knew that we had discussed with the client team what should be used as source, and it was the associate who should have taken the necessary steps to cite the source. But I quickly put this thought aside: I was the project manager, so whatever had happened was my responsibility. I strained my brain, trying to remember what we had agreed on at the time so that I could identify the sources I needed to check.

We had agreed with the client to base our sampling frame on an existing time-series project with the same client. Time-series projects run over an extended period of time, in this case about three years. We knew that the sampling frame was robust, as it was based on the Malaysian Department of Statistics (DOS) data and on syndicated studies that our company had run for those data points—studies that could not be otherwise obtained.[4] These statistics typically change every four years or so, and therefore the studies need to be refreshed periodically, so next I consulted the sampling frame of the original time-series project, as a simple reference point to test if my data or Conny's was the underlying issue. To my great relief, my data matched. But the moment of elation was short-lived. I scrolled down further, expecting to see a date stamp from around 2012, which was when the study had started, just two years prior to our study and thus within the acceptable or normal timeframe for official statistics availability. My heart skipped a beat: the year 2009 was printed in font nine italics underneath the table.

After a moment of disbelief, in which I kept asking myself how the still ongoing project could possibly be based on such an outdated sampling frame, I frantically went online to check the data directly from the DOS source. I felt it was absolutely critical to compare the latest figures with what I had at hand, to see how big a problem we were facing, how big the difference would be over the years.

As I waited for the data to load, I silently willed the situation to reveal itself as some kind of misunderstanding. My first instinct was to call the associate and clarify my thoughts step by step, finding out

---

[4] Syndicated studies are studies run by the company itself for syndicated resale, rather than client proprietary studies such as our project, in which the data obtained is the intellectual property of the client.

if there was anything I remembered wrongly, some miracle salvation I had overlooked. But I knew that before reaching out to any third party, I needed to be crystal clear on all the available data points. Soon, I had all evidence collected, and my frantic searches kept coming back with only one, repetitive answer: I had carelessly allowed the sampling frame of our study to rely on an existing study, without first verifying the date of the original study. I had simply assumed that the original study had been based on the latest census data.

I was now faced with a simple choice: hide my findings and reassure Jerry, Conny, and the team that our data was accurate and reflective, citing convincing rationales and reminding them that since it used proprietary data, they weren't allowed in any case to make use of the study; or swallow the bitter pill and admit not only to Jerry, but to Conny and the regional managing director that I had made a catastrophic error in sampling the entire study. The mistake could easily have been rectified had I only re-weighted the data earlier, but now, after so much time had passed, all the client deliverables would have to be redone, the data rerun, and statements issued to rectify the published data. In my mind, it was clear that Jerry would side with Conny and cite his previous request to be "kept abreast of developments," which I had not honored thoroughly. Most importantly, though by coming clean, we would demonstrate our integrity and commitment to transparency, the confession would have a serious impact on our overall relationship with the client, affecting not only this study, but others as well. My career would be over, of that I was certain. The person who never really fit in to begin with, from that early Monday morning training, until so many years later. I watched the cycle come to a close before my eyes.

As I was typing my email, trying to maintain a factual and concise tone, tears welled up in my eyes. I finished writing, read and re-read the email multiple times, and then let my finger linger over the "send" button. Was I ready to admit defeat? To break my pride and open myself up to criticism?

This professional crisis was what led me to my third insight, that in life, there are no villains, there are no heroes, only people who make choices based on the information available to them at the time, their circumstances at the time, and on their personal motivations. Wanting to be liked is programmed into our DNA for survival. But the extent to which we are willing to bend our own moral principles to elicit this liking is guided by our own moral compass. Perhaps on that fateful Monday morning of the training, had I chosen a different seat, things would have turned out very differently? Perhaps not at all. Maybe if my manager had not left the team and Jerry never became my boss, things would have been different, but then again, perhaps not. Perhaps if I had been more careful, things would have been different. Of that I am sure.

As professionals, we ought to strive always to make fair and honest decisions. To not ourselves be guided by emotions or personal preferences when possible. Especially when we are deprived of all facts, we ought to strive to make the best decisions possible with the information at hand at the time. Often these are the hard choices, and they teach us lessons in humility: after all, nobody is perfect, whether if they are part of the "Teflon Gang" or not. But our faith in our own ability to follow the right path will propel us to the next achievements, giving us increasing confidence to take on greater challenges, face bigger adversities.

At every stage of our lives, we feel that the ethical or otherwise challenges we face are the most profound and earth-shattering we will ever face. We can't imagine emerging intact on the other side of the moral storm we find ourselves in. That day, I thought my life as a professional in market research was about to cease. Like a grade-schooler who tries to arrange the teacher's books and ends up breaking an ornament by mistake, we struggle within ourselves whether to fess up or pray that we won't be found out. A profound, stomach-dropping, gut-wrenching feeling of despair sets in. Surely the "others"—the elders, the authority figures—will never forgive us for our innocent transgression. We want to avoid punishment, the loss of love, and the diminution of our self-esteem at all costs. Do we keep quiet, deny what happened, lie? How will we feel about ourselves afterwards?

In the moment, these questions seem unanswerable. But, as we have all experienced, when we emerge victoriously on the other side of the storm, we find ourselves transformed. We are stronger, more capable, and more adept in difficult situations. Those others, instead of shunning us, treat us with more trust and respect. If we allow them to, we can overcome those snap-judgement first impressions, and grow together to become better people together. Life teaches us lessons in humility whether we want it to or not.

Like any muscle, our moral code must be flexed and trained in order to become strong and healthy. After facing an ethical crisis, we will find that we have grown. It does not require saving a life or falling prey to some big misfortune to apply ethics, the little ways we engage with fellow people every day, can make a big difference. And that is what life is about, every day.

| Chapter 7 |
My Leadership Journey

Peter K.H. Law

● ● ●

I was a last minute inclusion for the ALE program called "Case Method Teaching: A Way Forward for Effective Pedagogy." The program was not my first choice, but looking back, I would have regretted tremendously if I had not attended it. Learning from professors from Harvard, a world-leading institution known for pioneering the case method of teaching, was the best way for me to learn and understand more about the pedagogy. My goal when I began the program was to be able to return to my workplace and help to design the learning program there, using similar approaches. I also wanted to learn writing simple cases to enhance my own teaching and learning.

I had told myself, "Just go back to university, keep an open mind, and check this out." I did not realize that the classes would start at 8 a.m. every day. I also did not realize that there would be so many cases to read. I was quite unprepared for Day 1, but I quickly understood that if I did not do the homework and read all the cases, I would accomplish nothing. The journey of the week-long program was not an easy one, waking up at 5:30 in the morning is not something I do all the time—but the preparation and the sharing that ensued among the participants were immensely enriching, especially with the cases that revolved around ethics, power, and decision making. The experience led me to contemplate whether I have done the right things thus far in my personal and professional life. It also kept me wondering if God had particular plans for me, and if I had lived up to my parents' expectations as well as my Catholic upbringing. The more I read about the cases, the more I reflected, and my thoughts brought me back to the past, some two decades ago, when I began my quest for leadership.

I was born and raised in a poor family in Sarawak, East Malaysia, with many siblings, and my childhood and adolescence did not give me any exposure to luxury. I was frequently referred to by teachers, classmates, and friends as "kampung boy"—village boy. My father was the sole breadwinner of the family, and worked 365 days a year, the only exception was during Chinese New Year and the times when he was sick. My family's income was so low that we did not have the opportunity to grow up like urban children. My father's work required him to travel daily, and he often made just enough to put food on the table. On days when his income was insufficient, we ate plain porridge with sugar or soy sauce for our meals. But seeing our father work so hard for his whole life motivated us to do part-time jobs to cover our own expenses, even when we were young. I helped my father collect wood for cooking. We also grew our own vegetables. Despite being poor, my parents were adamant that all of us needed to be properly educated; more importantly, they raised us with hardwired moral values so that we would not be a burden to the family.

I was brought up in an environment whereby Catholic doctrines and practices took precedence in many aspects of our lives. All of my siblings and I took up leadership roles in various groups and subgroups in the church. The Catholic upbringing taught us to do good, and I feel I now have a natural tendency to contribute to society. On top of that, my parents' consistent message to us was "Study hard and get a secure job, or else you will be a garbage collector." They also told us that we must always "do the right thing." My parents regarded good education as the only way to get us out of the poverty cycle. As they did not have the opportunity to further their studies when they were young, they insisted that all of their children go to college or at least complete high school. I still remember what my father told me, "You can't be working harder than me, hoping to earn a better living, right?" My parents' views on education were similar to Plutarch's statement—"Education is not the filling of a pail, but the lighting of a fire." After many years, I still admire their outlook; they lit my intellectual fire and encouraged me to improve myself every day.

After high school, I wanted to pursue my studies abroad. Just like many of my friends who continued their studies either in Peninsular Malaysia or overseas, I was eager to pursue further studies in Europe. Soon realizing how burdensome this was to my father, my older brother advised that I do it locally. My brother offered to support me financially—on one condition: I had to earn my first-year tuition fees. In order to do that, I needed to get a job and save enough money for the first year of college.

Key Lessons from My First Job

The first job I took up was at a timber trading company, which paid me very well, better than what most of my peers were paid. But it wasn't my dream job, or the kind of life that I wanted to pursue. The job required me to deal with the Forestry Department and the Customs Department, exporting round logs and processed timber to various countries, including Japan, Korea, and China. I witnessed rampant unethical practices amongst the timber exporters in their dealings with these departments. I knew the practices were not right, but I was too young and powerless to fight the system and the practices. Corruption was the norm back then, as far as I knew. The timber exporters were willing to pay cash for speedy documentation and positive inspections.

At that time, I often wondered if I should stay in the job and continue to operate in this kind of environment, earning a good income but being exposed to corruption. My upbringing made me think that I should strive, as always, to do the right thing. The moment my savings reached the amount needed for my first-year college tuition fees, I started applying to various colleges in Peninsular Malaysia. I was accepted into a local private college, and my aim was to enroll quickly and leave my hometown to pursue my tertiary education. By doing that, I would escape from the unethical practices of the timber trade, which went against my moral values.

I was still naive then and thought that the outside world was idealistic, that after I had moved on I would not have to deal with those issues anymore. Only much later did I realize that I was wrong to have such an assumption, that unless someone stands up and corrects the wrong, nothing will change. At the time, I was still under the impression that, with education, I could make a difference and change the world. The reality, however, is that even highly educated people often wreak havoc in society, committing fraud and unethical practices.

A Word from My Father: Be a Good Son

On the day when I departed for Peninsular Malaysia, both of my parents took me to the airport. My father is a man of few words. In the departure lounge, he uttered the phrase "Be a good son" and handed me my suitcase. Brief though it was, however, that phrase has been my key motivation in the last two decades of my life. I was determined to work hard and make him proud of me. I wasn't brave enough to ask him what he meant in the departure lounge, but I suppose he wanted me to study hard, get a good job, and live a life doing the right thing and practicing good moral values, the values that both he and my mother instilled in me. I have kept this silent promise to my parents throughout the years. His four-word phrase lives deep within me. Every time I feel overwhelmed by challenges in life, I pray to God for wisdom. I also try, with all my thoughts, words, and actions, to "be a good son." It has been one of the most meaningful things my father ever said to me.

In my early student days, my life was simple because I wasn't in the position to make any big decisions for people other than myself. My choices affected only myself and, at most, my family. After graduating from college, however, I started working, and as I progressed into a team leader role, my decision making became more important in other people's lives.

At an early stage of my career, I was given the opportunity to work abroad—an opportunity that was envied by many of my peers. Soon, I ran into a situation in which I had to decide whether to go with the flow, following a tradition of petty corruption, or do the right thing. When I went on a staff recruitment assignment in Sri Lanka, job-seeking candidates offered me many gifts and favors with the hope that I would hire them. Some of the candidates who were not successful in the interviews offered me gifts and favors so that I would change my mind and choose them for the jobs. Such inducement was very tempting. When I went back to Sri Lanka for my second assignment, the job-seeking candidates also offered me bribes. Every time I encountered such situations, I would refer to my father's advice to "be a good son" and to abide by my religious upbringing. So I would only hire qualified candidates who met the criteria for the jobs.

My Leadership Journey, Lesson 2.0: My First Job Abroad

When Professor Kenneth Winston and Professor Mathias Risse brought up "The Prison Master's Dilemma" case study in the ALE Case Method program, the case kept reminding me of my first job, with the timber trading company, and my working experience in China. In "The Prison Master's Dilemma," the protagonist, Khalil, faces a challenge that affects his personal integrity. His parents taught him to despise corrupt and unjust behavior, but during his stay in Europe, he learns that corruption is more than just a monetary transaction. When he returns to his own country and starts working, he finds himself in an environment in which bribery and corruptions are the norm. Like me, Khalil must face a conflict between his moral convictions and his official duties.

In May 1998, during the peak of the first Asian financial crisis, I worked as the Senior Human Resources Manager of a theme park in Qingdao, China, which was developed by a Singapore-based company. There, I was entrusted to hire and train staff. Again, I was offered many bribes, as jobs were scarce in a country of over a billion people. In June, unemployment in China among recent graduates was so high that when the company hosted a walk-in interview session, the ratio between our vacancies and the number of applicants was at least 1:10, giving me a lot of choices. The fresh graduates were willing to do almost anything to land a job, including offering bribes and getting someone in a position of power to influence the hiring decision. On many occasions, they offered me favors and cash so that I would "close one eye" and accept an unsuitable or unqualified candidate—but I always chose to do the right thing, as I was paid to deliver value to the company. On one occasion, I was offered a tour package if I accepted the relative of a senior government official who did not meet the minimum criteria for the job. It was a tough call for me: on the one hand, I needed to hire the best and most qualified candidate, but, on the other hand, I didn't want to offend the government official, for fear of having the company's operating license suspended. Choosing not to offer the unqualified candidate a job gave me a lot of sleepless nights, but I knew it was the right thing to do. Not long after the incident, several spot checks were carried out by the local authorities. Our operations were delayed, and some were suspended. I could not be sure that these actions were linked to the decisions I had made in the stringent hiring process, but I thought it was probable.

In early August 1998, my work visa expired and I was worried that I might be put into detention, as that was how the communist authorities operated then. When I spoke to my Government Liaison Officer, he only smiled and said, "Let me see what I can do. You might need to come with me to the police station tomorrow." To make things worse, my colleague told me that an overstay without a valid visa is a severe offence; he had never encountered such a situation before, since usually people seek extensions before their visas expire.

The next day, when we went to the police station to make the report and seek an extension, my colleague assured me that he would be able to get at least a thirty-day extension of my stay that would give me sufficient time to prepare for my departure. That assurance gave me a lot of relief, but I soon started to wonder how he would fulfill his promise. At the police station, I was questioned by a policeman who assured me that his boss would be able to help; he referred my case to the officer in charge. He then led my colleague into the officer's office for a separate discussion. I was left alone, waiting in agony and worrying about the consequences I would have to face.

Half an hour later, my colleague returned with a big smile on his face. I was profoundly relieved: I knew that he had "solved" my worries. Later, I learned from him that "In China, money can do wonders. Without money, everything is impossible." Heading back home, I wondered what I would have done had I was there alone? Would I have bribed him or have chosen to be extradited?

In the summer of 1998, my company opened a world-class theme park. The business was doing fine, but my finance colleague told me that our cash flow was not in good shape. I wondered what went wrong. By the end of summer, I had a rude awakening: one of my finance staff was arrested and detained by the local authorities. I was told that she had been arrested for helping the director bring $100,000 in cash to Singapore. Apparently, this was done regularly: a board member would transport the cash in a briefcase to Singapore, thus leaving the company short of cash and unable to pay vendors and its most important asset, its two thousand employees.

After much "negotiation" with the local authorities, my colleague was released with a warning that she must be available for further investigations. I was not aware if any bribe had been offered for her release. Several expatriates gathered and discussed what we should do to safeguard our young colleague. We knew that we needed to do the right thing to secure her safe return to Singapore. Taking swift actions, some of my senior colleagues made the needful arrangements and sent her off to Beijing, where she could catch the earliest possible flight out of China to avoid detention. We all knew that such offences led to severe jail sentences in China. The incident reminds me of a book entitled *Leadership Without Easy Answers* (1994), written by Ronald Heifetz. As Heifetz predicted, there have been many tough lessons in my leadership journey, and no easy answers.

In this case, I learned that a selfish leader can make or break an organization. After the incident, I was faced with a choice: leave the organization or stay and fight the malpractices. I knew that doing the latter would mean not only going against my paymaster, but also becoming an odd man out in the organization. I was in a foreign land, facing an uncertain and ambiguous situation all by myself. I thus told my Malaysian boss that if the company needed to reduce its expatriate headcount, I would be happy to return to Malaysia after getting the payment of my outstanding salary. A month later, my boss gave me a letter informing me that my contract was ending. I gladly accepted the news, not realizing that I wouldn't be receiving any of my well-deserved three months outstanding salary. Later, I fought for my outstanding pay, but to no avail. That was when I made a pledge to myself that if one day I reached a position of power, I would always correct the wrong and do the right thing. Since then, I have felt more committed than ever to my parents' values of honesty and integrity.

My Leadership Journey, Lesson 3.0: Advocating Doing the Right Thing

I have faced many obstacles throughout my career. Often, I had to decide between doing the right thing, which would require me to speak out, and going with the flow, accepting that I do not have the power to make a difference. When Professor Winston and Mr. Hungsoo S. Kim made reference to Heifetz's advice to move back and forth between "the dance floor" and "the balcony," I remembered another of Heifetz's statements, that "leadership arouses passion" because it engages our values. This thought made me ask myself, "Am I living up to my values?" Heifetz goes on to suggest that leadership means mobilizing people to tackle tough problems. Today, as injustice continues to persist around the world, it is easy to get disheartened or lose motivation. I often wonder if I can make a difference in addressing the inequality occurring around me. Should I stay quiet in the face of injustice? I was lost and still do not have a clear answer. Indeed, leadership never provides such easy answers!

When Professor Risse brought up the "Aung San Suu Kyi" case for discussion, many in the class thought that the Burmese stateswoman was not a good leader; I was one of the few who advocated in her favor as a leader. She was offered a chance to leave the country to visit her dying husband, with the knowledge that she might not be granted a re-entry, but she chose to stay put, thus missing her husband's last moments. I would argue that she is a good leader because she did not abandon her people. Her case made me wonder if I had done the right thing by leaving my first job and not fighting the "normative environment" of unethical practices. On the other hand, Heifetz argues that "Leaders are always failing somebody." Walking away from my first job and leaving the issue to others who were in the position to deal with it made sense, since I did not hold any power to make the change. Still, my moral conscience told me otherwise. How could I resolve this dichotomy? Similarly, it seemed logical that Malaysians should leave the common problems that confront the community and country to their elected Parliamentarians, but Heifetz and Marty Linsky suggest in *Leadership on the Line* (2002) that "when people look to authorities for easy answers to adaptive challenges, they end up with dysfunction." So the ALE case method program made me realize that I need to make the active choice: to right the wrong and speak up about the most pressing issues facing our society.

Heifetz also claims that "leadership is both active and reflective; one has to alternate between participating and observing" (1994). Recently, I have chosen the observing role rather than a participating one. During the program, I experienced many difficult moments when I reflected on what I had done in the last two decades of my life. I have had my fair share of both disappointments and successes, but my reflection always triggered these two questions: "Am I doing the right thing?" and "Am I the leader who is always failing somebody?"

In my leadership journey, I have been experiencing all the ups and downs in being true to myself. I have been fortunate to get promoted almost once every two years at all the companies that I have worked with. It was even more meaningful when my bosses told me that they were pleased with my work ethic as well as my open and honest communication with them. Hence, I truly believe that living a life of integrity will eventually help me in my career progression.

Leadership Lessons Learned: My Future!

As the week progressed, the ALE program became more and more intense. My mind was loaded with unanswered questions: What do I do best? What am I able to do? What can I do to make a difference? What difference can I make to keep myself happy while "being a good son" to my father? What does happiness mean to me? What small things can I change in my current role to create lasting positive effects in other people's lives? What do I need to sacrifice to make myself happy? These and dozens of other questions crowded together in my mind.

As the French novelist Anatole France once said, "To accomplish great things, we must dream as well as act." I finally decided to write this chapter, hoping that I would live up to my promise to Mr. Kim—to share my knowledge and experience with others. I faced many challenges while writing this chapter, including disciplining myself to sit down and put my thoughts into words. But, with a lot of encouragement from my wife, I have finally achieved my dream of writing my first book chapter!

After much pondering for the last three weeks, I have realized that I am happiest when I can be myself, doing what I enjoy, without needing to put on a mask. I am also happiest when I can speak up for the underprivileged, marginalized, neglected, and underrepresented people. I have come to the conclusion that if I can create an environment in which people have the opportunity to learn, develop, and thrive, I have the ability to make a lasting positive impact on people's lives. When I create such opportunities within an organization, institution, or society, I am giving people the chance and skills to grow. When that happens, I am improving the financial status of individuals and, in a nutshell, growing the economic pie that we all share. In other words, I am like Ann in the "Women in the Corridor" case that was taught during the ALE program—doing small things to make a difference.

In my current role, I have created a simple yet engaging platform for youth to come together. In order for young people to form a formidable force to shape the nation's future, I strongly believe that they need to be given opportunities to learn and improve themselves. Many leaders of the Baby Boomer generation feel that Generation Y and Millennials are inexperienced and thus, should not be given leadership roles. I believe otherwise, and I have established two 'Personal & Leadership Development' programs for a pool of talented youth. In these programs, they go to a setting that requires them to interact with different personalities, in hopes of dispelling their self-limiting beliefs and take action to improve their lives. We provided them with coaching sessions over a period of twenty-four to thirty-six months, and I spent a great deal of time mentoring them. Over the last seven years, I have given many hours to these youth because I believe that they are Malaysia's future. Working with them gives me a sense of meaning in life; I know I can make a difference in encouraging them to be the people they have always wanted to be. The work is my way of giving back to my community. I can't compare myself with Henry in the case of "A Gift of Life," in which he breaks all the rules to save a life, saving a baby's life rather than completing the abortion as he was instructed to do. Although it was not a life-and-death situation, I did break some rules to "save" some of the youth I've worked with. While breaking rules is usually uncommon in the commercial enterprise, I decided to do the unconventional approach including having crucial conversations to encourage young staff to leave the organization if they can find another company that can provide the platform to unlock their full potential. I even recommended other suitable organizations if my company is unable to fulfill their dreams. I also encouraged the young generation to challenge the status quo within the company as it will create constructive debates to push other colleagues including line managers to perform better.

In the course of my work, I have been fortunate enough to meet Rajeev Peshawaria, who authored the book *Too Many Bosses, Too Few Leaders* (2011). Peshawaria argues that many people act and behave like bosses but only a few live up to their roles as leaders. Every time I see the book on my shelf, it reminds me to go out and be a leader. As stated in many of the cases discussed in the ALE program, leadership requires courage. A leader cannot hide or stay away, embracing the theory of "out of sight, out of mind." Often, I do not have the courage to right the wrong—I am scared to endanger the safety of my family members. This fear often forces me to compromise, and in the end I walk away feeling miserable. I keep asking myself, "Where can I get the courage to do what is right?" To this day, I am still searching for an answer. Perhaps the ALE program is the kick-start I need to learn how to have courage.

"The Prison Master's Dilemma" case taught me to stay true to my beliefs. The protagonist, Khalil, endures many painful experiences, and in the end he decides to do what is right. The case made me wonder: if I had stayed in my job at the timber trading company, what kind of person would I be now? Would I be contributing to the unethical practices in my community, or would I be standing tall and advocating doing the right thing to the many young leaders of the future? "The Prison Master's Dilemma" encouraged me to nurture the younger generation to become effective and ethical leaders for tomorrow. The world is becoming more globalized and I strongly believe that young Malaysians should step up to the plate to contribute to the country's development. Therefore, I have chosen to coach our youth, encouraging them to embrace strong moral values.

The ripple effect can be powerful. If, in the next year, I recruit five more people to join me in doing something to make a difference in society, and they replicate my actions by recruiting five more people, we would have reached 9,765,625 people within the next ten years! Perhaps I am still as idealistic as I was when I first left my hometown two decades ago. But with ten million change agents in Malaysia by 2025, I am sure we will be able to make significant changes to every aspect of life in this beautiful country. In the spirit of "Merdeka" or independence, I believe that if every Malaysian put in a small effort to overcome the country's challenges, we would have a better Malaysia!

Of course, it will not be easy. For example, if people are brought up in an environment whereby unethical practices are deemed acceptable, it can be almost impossible for them to learn what is right and what is wrong. Under such circumstances, you cannot expect them to do the right thing. However, if you take these people out of their original environments and allow them to experience and learn the right things, their futures will be different. Just as Khalil learns the meaning of corruption after his studies in Europe, others can learn about honest practices by experiencing them firsthand.

So where do I start? I am now making a pledge that I will start spreading positive changes in both my community and my workplace. I know that it will be tough to get started before gaining the needful momentum, but I am determined to begin right away. Often, doing the right thing does not give us comfort; we are often discriminated against just because we are standing on the opposite side of the majority. Also, as the author Somerset Maugham pointed out, "The unfortunate thing about this world is that good habits are so much easier to give up than bad ones." I therefore urge all the leaders out there to not give up and to continue working for a better tomorrow. Tomorrow will not get better unless we start making changes today. We cannot be selfish and subscribe to the WIIFM culture—i.e. What's In It For Me? Rather, we should ask what we can do for others. I was confronted with many such situations in dealing with various authorities over the last two decades, but I am proud to say that I was able to do the right thing—and as the Italian designer Massimo Vignelli once said, "If you do it right, it will live forever."

It has been a rough and rocky journey over the past twenty years, as I tried to become who I am today. I have done my best to honor the silent promise I made to my parents. Even now, if someone were to ask me if I am a good leader, my answer would be, "Not yet"—but I am getting better by the day. In his poem, "Invictus," the Victorian poet, William Ernest Henley wrote, "I am the master of my fate, I am the captain of my soul." I am still trying hard to be the captain of my soul!

To sum up, I hope the leaders of today and tomorrow will go out and make the right decision as it will impact our future generation. God gave us a precious gift, the ability to make a choice—and the choices we make today dictate the life we live tomorrow. So make your choice now!

Part 4

Community Leadership: Leading Change for Organizational Renewal

| Chapter 8 |

Leveraging Uncertainty and Unlocking Your Best Self

Ida Fazila Ismail

● ● ●

Bee-ing Adaptable

Upon graduation, I joined a Malaysian public relations agency, which turned out to be the best training ground in shaping my career. One of our clients was an international consumer product company that specializes in oral health care. I worked closely with my superior to build awareness of the company's latest toothpaste that contains a natural ingredient created by bees and known for its antibacterial properties. Though there were just the two of us managing the account, we were determined to deliver the best results to our client. We wanted to create a buzz for the product launch and played around with the "bee" element. We explored the idea of getting a bee farmer to stage a Malaysia Book of Records attempt, by sitting with forty thousand bees for half an hour in an enclosed cubicle. It sounded crazy, but it was an outside-the-box idea that had the potential to generate an enormous amount of publicity. We sought the advice of a few experts to ensure that the idea was feasible. Our client agreed with the idea, and we began planning for the launch.

Then, just when I thought everything was under control, my superior told me that he would be out of the country for a month, beginning a few days before the launch. I was four months into my job, and I doubted myself: I didn't think I was prepared for the sudden responsibility of managing such a major work task. I was also worried about what my client would think of having a fresh graduate leading a critical event. However, my superior was confident that I would be able to pull it off. It felt like a huge burden, but I knew it was my duty to take ownership of the project.

I encountered hiccups along the way before the launch, and my superior feared for the worst while he was away, but I was in constant communication with him to ensure that we covered all the bases. Our main concerns were managing the logistics of bringing the huge amount of bees safely to the venue, as the bee farmer was based in the southern Malaysian state of Johor, a four-hour drive away from Kuala Lumpur; maintaining the bee farmer's safety when staging the record attempt; and ensuring that the bees would not escape from the enclosed cubicle and sting members of the public witnessing the event!

In the end, the launch went well. The client was happy and the event was free of any unwanted incidents, thanks to everyone involved, including my colleagues, who contributed to the success of the project. We had a good media turnout at the event and received positive coverage in major newspapers and TV stations. Even today, it remains one of my most memorable work experiences and I am thankful to my superior for giving me the opportunity to learn and grow.

As clichéd as it may sound, if we see challenges as opportunities, we can become stronger and more competent for the next time life throws us a curveball. The key is to be agile and adaptable in order to survive in an ever-changing environment. Bees diligently seek pollen and nectar as food for their colony, and they are able to survive almost everywhere except areas such as Antarctica, where there are no flowers that they can feed on. I think that we should emulate bees' perseverance, agility, and adaptability to survive in our fast-moving world.

Experiences such as the one described above, as well as current events happening in the world, have shaped the way I think and react to change. For now, I am still learning and working out my own kinks. In the process, I have realized that everyone has a voice and can make a difference in the world. You do not have to be rich or belong to an exclusive group of prominent and high-rung professionals to initiate change. I strongly believe that everyday people are the most powerful agents of change. Others may put a damper on your efforts as you navigate life to find answers and solutions, but you should not allow their petty gripes to affect you.

A quote from a famous Apple TV advertisement, aptly titled "Think Different," cleverly sums up my view on this: "Here's to the crazy ones. The misfits. The rebels. The troublemakers. The round pegs in the square holes. The ones who see things differently. They're not fond of rules. And they have no respect for the status quo. You can quote them, disagree with them, glorify or vilify them. About the only thing you can't do is ignore them. Because they change things. They push the human race forward. And while some may see them as the crazy ones, we see genius. Because the people who are crazy enough to think they can change the world are the ones who do."

A Newfound Understanding of Leadership

Shortly after joining CALI Malaysia, I had the opportunity to participate in one of its ALE programs, "Leading Change for Organizational Renewal," led by Professor Dean Williams, Adjunct Lecturer in Public Policy for the Center for Public Leadership, Harvard Kennedy School; Mr. Hungsoo S. Kim, President of CALI; and Mr. John Lim, Managing Director of CALI Boston.

As an introvert, I am a reserved and private person who usually prefers to be in the background. I hadn't really bothered about leadership prior to joining the three-day program. My definition of leadership up to that point was leading a team of followers to achieve a shared goal. However, I was keen to learn what the program was all about, as it aimed to offer participants an insight into an adaptive leadership framework that encourages creative and analytical thinking, and flexibility in facing changes at the workplace. This adaptive leadership framework is taught at Harvard, including the Kennedy School. It inspires leaders to be change agents, to cross boundaries, and to build bridges in order to pave the path for growth, as well as nurturing strong collaborations with relevant stakeholders to overcome challenges effectively. Professor Williams is an authority on adaptive leadership and change. His courses at Harvard are among the most popular at the university. Hence, I was looking forward to the program.

Professor Williams kick-started his session with a simple and straightforward question: "What is leadership?" I was sure that all forty-four participants in the room, including me, were confident of our answers, most of which were along the lines of "a leader is someone who leads a group of people toward a common target." Those who raised their hands gave similar answers. We were surprised to learn that our definition of leadership was quite outdated. Professor Williams explained to us that the old way of leading is no longer relevant in today's ever-evolving world. He added that, in a globalized world, people are becoming more and more interconnected, regardless of different time zones and geographical locations. As the world becomes more complex at a rapid speed, leaders must be well-equipped, fast, and flexible in adapting to change. They have no choice but to face reality, adopt fresh perspectives, learn new approaches, and implement bold actions to overcome pressing workplace issues. If they do not, they risk of being left behind in our competitive world.

Professor Williams further explained that people are naturally tribal and tend to congregate with those who have similar characteristics. But the tribal model of leadership, which entails getting people to follow you and do what they are told to do, does not work anymore. According to Professor Williams, becoming leaders of the 21st century means we need to be change agents who can cross boundaries and mobilize people to face challenges head-on in times of trouble. He reminded us that every challenge is an opportunity to learn something that fosters creative thinking and enables us to find innovative solutions to a problem.

What caught my attention most was when Professor Williams mentioned that, in today's world, power is widely distributed and no single person is all-powerful. This means that everyone can be a leader, with the ability to create positive change and influence the complex system that we live in. After listening to Professor Williams, I realized that everyone has the capacity to become change agents, even in the most conservative environments. And these change agents are the earth shakers. They shake the ground and stir people to think differently about the world around them and to take actions to make it a better place.

Breaking Barriers, Initiating Change

Professor Williams' definition of leadership reminded me of my career in public relations, in which I worked with a number of health and pharmaceutical clients, and was privileged to have collaborated with many inspiring Malaysians in the fields of medicine and science. One of them was Professor Adeeba Kamarulzaman, a prominent Malaysian figure in the field of HIV/AIDS. Besides being the Dean of the Faculty of Medicine, and Professor of Medicine and Infectious Diseases at the University of Malaya, Professor Adeeba is also the Chairman of the Malaysian AIDS Foundation and a Co-Chair of the WHO Technical and Strategic Advisory Committee on HIV. She played a crucial role in initiating the Malaysian Government's shift in drug policies, which saw the implementation of harm reduction programs, including the methadone drug substitution therapy (MDST) in 2005 to treat heroin addiction and control HIV/AIDS in Malaysia.[1]

Working on a project with Professor Adeeba as well as other experts in the field to generate awareness of the MDST exposed me to the myths and realities of drug addiction in Malaysia. I learned that the majority of people infected with HIV in Malaysia are drug addicts who contracted the virus through contaminated needles and syringes. Methadone is taken orally and eliminates needle and syringe

---

[1] "Prof. Adeeba Kamarulzaman," International Doctors for Healthier Drug Policies. Accessed December 13, 2016. http://idhdp.com/en/about/prof-adeeba-kamarulzaman.aspx.

sharing, thus reducing the number of new HIV infections. Regrettably, the MDST has received a great deal of criticism. Traditional conservative views on drug addiction have spurred misconceptions about the MDST due to the nature of the program. The MDST does not simply substitute one drug for another. It offers a legally accessible and medically safe treatment to drug users. However, as it involves a marginalized community, other people tend to gravitate toward a judgmental moral standpoint when discussing it, instead of looking at the big picture. Many do not realize that drug addiction is not merely a social problem, but a chronic medical disease that should be treated like any other illness.

Together with her colleagues in the field, Professor Adeeba broke boundaries, halting maladaptive practices that impeded people's ability to face the problematic reality and changing public perceptions of drug addiction and harm reduction programs. Before the Malaysian Government endorsed the harm reduction programs, Malaysia was home to one of South-Eastern Asia's most explosive epidemics of HIV infection, with almost half of all new HIV infections in the country occurred among injecting drug users.[2] Prior to the introduction of the MDST, Malaysia's portfolio of drug addiction treatment was under the Ministry of Home Affairs, which applied an abstinence model, using long-term institutional incarceration as its primary approach in handling drug users.[3] This approach, emphasizing total abstinence,

---

[2] Wickersham, Jeffrey, et al., "Implementing Methadone Maintenance Treatment in Prisons in Malaysia," *Bulletin of the World Health Organization*, 91, no. 2 (February 2013): 124-129, doi: 10.2471/BLT.12.109132.

[3] Vicknasingam, B and Mazlan, Mahmud, "Malaysian Drug Treatment Policy: An Evolution from Total Abstinence to Harm Reduction," *Malaysian Anti-Drugs Journal*. Accessed December 14, 2016. http://www.adk.gov.my/html/

was proven to be unsuccessful, with high relapse rates of 70 and 90 percent within the first year following discharge; in other words, many drug users ended up going back to their old habits.[4] However, the pilot MDST project in 2005 saw excellent retention rates of up to 90 percent in the first year, a huge accomplishment when benchmarked against the World Health Organization's retention rate standards of 55 to 60 percent.[5] The MDST and the provision of clean needles to drug users have successfully averted 12,653 HIV infections since their introduction, saving the Malaysian Government RM47.1 million, and they are expected to avert 23,241 new HIV infections and savings of RM210 million by 2023.[6] The Malaysian Government's adoption of the MDST, against much public opposition, and the success of the harm reduction strategy were both important victories for Professor Adeeba and her colleagues.

As a humble leader, Professor Adeeba acts without regard for her own well-being and gives credit where credit is due. She draws strength and inspiration from the people she works with, including the government, non-governmental organizations, the medical frater-

---

pdf/jurnal/2008/5.pdf.

[4] Ibid.

[5] Paul, Ravichandran, "Clearing the Air Over Methadone Therapy for Addicts," *Bernama*. May 14, 2009. http://www.bernama.com/bernama/state_news/bm/news.php?id=410979&cat=ut.

[6] "Malaysia's Public Health Policies Assisting People Who Inject Drugs Are Found to Avert New HIV Infections, Save Lives and Reduce Health Care Costs, According to A New Study Funded by the World Bank," The World Bank. December 18, 2013. http://www.worldbank.org/en/news/press-release/2013/12/18/malaysias-public-health-policies-assisting-people-who-inject-drugs-to-avert-new-hiv-infections-according-to-a-new-study-funded-by-the-world-bank.

nity, educational institutions, drug users, people living with HIV, the media, and her local community in her bid to advocate the research, prevention, and treatment of HIV/AIDS in Malaysia.[7] Professor Adeeba transcends boundaries by engaging with people from every facet of society, nurturing conditions that cultivate collaborative problem solving. Her success exemplifies the virtues of change agents who understand the need to cross boundaries to accomplish their goals, as they believe that issues cannot be solved in isolation.

Despite the success rate, public stigma and discrimination surrounding the harm reduction programs remain, and the law-and-order approach still reigns. Professor Adeeba stressed the importance of urgent change because, if we maintain the status quo of arresting drug users and sending them to prisons or rehabilitation centers, it will prevent them from leading normal and independent lives, contributing to the community, and gaining access to proper treatment.[8] She believes that it is imperative for every party to rethink the approach to drug policies and to manage the issue from a public health perspective in order to effectively tackle the war on drug addiction and the spread of HIV/AIDS.[9]

Professor Williams mentioned that being a change agent means you have to build bridges between divided groups, in order to get people to communicate with each other and to resolve any misunder-

---

[7] "'Meaningful Award' for Prof Adeeba," *The Star Online*. April 26, 2015. http://www.thestar.com.my/news/education/2015/04/26/meaningful-award-for-prof-adeeba/.

[8] Balasegaram, Mangai, "Huge Shift Needed in Global Drug Policy," Star2.com. March 28, 2016. http://www.star2.com/living/2016/03/28/health-experts-huge-shift-needed-in-global-drug-policy/.

[9] Ibid.

standings, thus establishing trust and compassion. Many leaders tend to overlook the value of seeing the bigger picture. It is crucial to put yourself in the other parties' shoes in order to know what they are doing and to understand their feelings and circumstances. This practice will push leaders to develop humility and empathy, which in turn will encourage them to take a step back and reflect. Looking at situations from a different viewpoint will allow leaders to see the whole picture and effectively guide their teams toward a common objective.

Professor Adeeba's leadership style in dealing with drug addiction and HIV/AIDS holistically, as a doctor and an advocate, perfectly reflects the qualities of a 21st century leader. Her hard work, passion, and dedication have also reshaped my view of female leadership; she has inspired me to commit to building knowledge for the betterment of humankind instead of concentrating on women's ability to break the glass ceiling or to create a business empire.

Professor Williams' session was both refreshing and intellectually stimulating. I now believe that all of us can make a difference in the volatile world we live in. I also learned that we should recognize leadership moments in every situation and turn them into opportunities, orchestrating interventions that challenge the existing situation and inspiring people to make positive social change. That is what leadership is all about.

The Best Birthday Gift Ever

Throughout the ALE program, I realized that the leadership lessons we learned could be applied in every area of life, not just in the workplace. As I reflected on the challenges that I have faced and overcome, I remembered that at one point, I went through a life-changing phase that forced me to adapt to unexpected changes.

Five years ago, I fell sick and underwent a fairly routine surgical procedure, one day after my birthday. At the time, I thought God must have had a wonderful sense of humor for giving me this "birthday present." The surgery went well, but afterward, the "adventure" began. About a week after my surgery, I woke up one day feeling different, with mysterious health symptoms. I thought they were post-surgery complications or allergic reactions to my medications. I was worried, but I assumed that the symptoms would subside after a while. Alas, that did not happen. I then went to see my surgeon, but he could not provide a concrete answer. The incident led to a medical investigation along the lines of those in the TV show *House*, involving a series of visits to the hospital for tests and follow-ups, until finally, I received my diagnosis.

I was not prepared for the agonizing uncertainty of this process, and it slowly dawned upon me that despite all our planning, we are never really in control. When a crisis happens, there is no other way to face it except to adapt. Due to my condition, I was unable to do several things that I used to enjoy. Simple everyday tasks that I had taken for granted became challenges, and it was an uphill battle to navigate my life while dealing with the side effects of different medications, on top of holding a demanding full-time job. This situation lasted for two years. I had no choice but to re-evaluate my daily routine in order to cope with its difficulties. My struggles came to mind during Mr. Kim's session, in which he talked about "going on the balcony," a practice promoted by the renowned adaptive leadership expert, Ronald A. Heifetz. Mr. Kim encouraged us to apply the technique when facing a challenging situation, as it allows one to step back and reflect. By looking at their current situations "from a balcony," leaders can gain a different perspective on their own actions and the activities of the people around them.

After undergoing treatment, I am now in remission, and I have developed a new view and attitude toward life. Based on this experience, I feel that going through a personal adaptive challenge is similar to exercising leadership as a change agent. In both cases, one must face reality and deal with uncertainty as the norm, develop a big-picture mentality, and orchestrate a process of adaptive change to harness creative problem solving in times of adversity.

As surprising as it may sound, I am grateful for my illness. The experience taught me adaptability, humility, empathy, patience, and mindfulness. It was, indeed, the best birthday gift ever. One day, I hope to share my experience with those in a similar situation and help them go through their own health challenges.

The State of the World We Live In

Leaders deal with challenges in various ways. Professor Williams highlighted the importance of practicing real leadership, which mobilizes people to focus on the issue at hand and to solve the problem together, creating change by modifying their values, habits, and ways of thinking.

According to Professor Williams, the opposite of real leadership is counterfeit leadership, which uses the various powers of authority without wisdom: prominence (look to me), dominance (listen to me), and tribalizing (follow me and I will advance your interests). Counterfeit leaders cope with challenges by practicing common problem avoidance mechanisms, including getting people to avoid reality, pursuing decoy issues, holding on to the past, searching for quick fixes, scapegoating other groups, maintaining the existing culture of "that's the way we do it around here," promoting chimpanzee politics (in reference to the territorial boundary patrol behavior in chimpanzees in which authority figures within an organization see it as their responsibility to protect their group's boundaries and engage in confrontations with change agents that challenge the status quo), placing excessive dependence on authority to "show the way," playing the "attack and blame" game, killing the dissident voice, and buying into a delusional vision out of desperation. Counterfeit leadership prevents people from achieving change or abandoning wrong values and practices that hamper progress and produce no sustainable value. On this issue, the American scientist and author, Jared Diamond said that when there is an absence of real leadership, institutions persist in a state of mediocrity, breakdown, or collapse.

Listening to Professor Williams, I could not help but relate his ideas and principles on leadership to current world affairs. Donald Trump's surprise presidential victory sent shockwaves not only through the United States but across the world.[10] People worldwide were stunned that Trump's political rhetoric of hate won him the U.S. presidency, which led throngs of demonstrators to protest his victory across the U.S. The problem avoidance mechanism mentioned earlier can be clearly seen in Trump's campaign; some of the policies he en-

---

10 Flegenheimer, Matt and Barbaro, Michael, "Donald Trump Is Elected President in Stunning Repudiation of the Establishment," *The New York Times*. November 9, 2016. http://www.nytimes.com/2016/11/09/us/politics/hillary-clinton-donald-trump-president.html.

dorses may be relatively harmless in the short-term, but they will lead to significant damage in the long run. Until today, the U.S. has been divided into two camps, Trump and anti-Trump. Unfortunately, the situation is not getting any better, and Trump will need to address the challenge strategically, through adaptive leadership, if he wishes to see the country and its people prosper.

Current global events have ignited a profound sense of urgency for more change makers to step up to the plate and exercise real leadership, helping people make sense of what is happening in the world today and taking appropriate actions to address the challenges. Professor Williams explained that change agents are earth shakers who can generate sufficient disequilibrium to shake people out of their complacency and cultural habits, and start tackling the problem.

The #DeleteUber campaign demonstrates a powerful example of what change agents can accomplish. Trump's first week in office stirred a sudden political awakening and a surge of political activism that the world has not seen. The U.S. president's controversial travel ban that bars citizens of seven Muslim-majority countries from entering the U.S., as well as his immigration order that suspends the admission of refugees, triggered a grassroots movement of progressives not only in the U.S. but also across the globe. The issue sparked a boycott by New York taxi drivers at JFK Airport to object the president's decision.[11] However, Uber decided to continue its services at the airport, a move that angered protestors and grew into the #DeleteUber hashtag that quickly began trending worldwide and

---

11 Benen, Steve, "Progressive Activism Forces Uber CEO to Break with Trump," MSNBC.com. February 3, 2017. http://www.msnbc.com/rachel-maddow-show/progressive-activism-forces-uber-ceo-break-trump.

incited many customers to delete the ride-sharing app. Soon after the incident, Uber CEO, Travis Kalanick quit Trump's business advisory council following heavy criticism from the company's employees and customers.[12] U.S. District Court Judge, James Robart later blocked Trump's travel ban nationwide and a federal appeals court unanimously denied the president's request to reinstate the ban.[13]

This inspiring story exemplifies how change agents who exercise real leadership are capable of creatively and tactically creating disruptions that stir things up and mobilize people from the bottom up to drive positive change. Hence, we should never be afraid to be active global citizens. Instead, we should strive to look for ways to build a more inclusive and equitable world in order to positively influence our larger communities.

A Quiet Authority

I majored in Applied Entomology for my undergraduate degree, and one of my professors recommended that his students read *Silent Spring*, a book on the harmful long-term effects of misusing pesticides on the environment. The book, published in 1962, was written by Rachel Carson, a soft-spoken writer, scientist, and ecologist. She was a classic introvert who demonstrated few of the traits typically associated with leadership, such as charisma and aggressiveness.[14] Yet Car-

---

12 Ibid.
13 Almasy, Steve and Simon, Darran, "Timeline: How President Trump's Travel Ban Unraveled," CNN.com. February 10, 2017. http://edition.cnn.com/2017/02/10/us/trump-travel-ban-timeline/.
14 Koehn, Nancy, "From Calm Leadership, Lasting Change," *The New York Times*. October 27, 2012. http://www.nytimes.com/2012/10/28/business/

son broke the mold, and her book sparked the environmental movement by challenging the practices of the government, businesses, and agricultural scientists, as well as calling mankind to be responsible caretakers of the earth and its inhabitants.

The controversial *Silent Spring* became an instant best-seller and even caught the attention of President John F. Kennedy, who read it in 1962 and directed his Science Advisory Committee in the same year to study pesticide use. A year later, the Committee released a report that supported Carson's claims.[15]

Criticism is part and parcel of a leader's journey to spur change, and Carson was not without her critics. The chemical industry and some members of the government accused her of fear-mongering, but this did not stop her from courageously speaking her mind, stressing that humans are a vulnerable part of the natural world who are subject to the same damage as the rest of the ecosystem.[16] Despite criticism and the efforts to discredit her writing, Carson strongly believed in her book and stood her ground. She testified before Congress on pesticide use in 1963, with the hope of creating stricter environmental policies. A year later she died, at the age of fifty-six, following a long battle with breast cancer.

Several events, such as a California oil spill; a chemical fire on the Cuyahoga River in Cleveland, Ohio; and civic protests against napalm and Agent Orange, chemical weapons used in the Vietnam

---

rachel-carsons-lessons-50-years-after-silent-spring.html.
15 "The Consequences of Silent Spring," America's Story from America's Library. Accessed November 28, 2016. http://www.americaslibrary.gov/aa/carson/aa_carson_consequenc_1.html.
16 Lear, Linda, "The Life and Legacy of Rachel Carson," RachelCarson.org. 2015. http://www.rachelcarson.org/.

War, occurred in the late 1960s and confirmed Carson's warnings that man's efforts to master nature instead of being an equal part of the ecosystem threatened human existence.[17] *Silent Spring* is now considered to be the Bible of the environmental movement, and its impact was monumental.[18] The positive consequences of the book included the creation of the Environmental Protection Agency (EPA) in 1970, in response to mounting public concern; the banning of DDT in 1972, the pesticide that prompted Carson's research for *Silent Spring*; and the passing of the Clean Water Act in 1972 and the Endangered Species Act in 1973.[19]

I find Rachel Carson's life story immensely inspirational. Her story resonates strongly with me because it shows that everyone, regardless of background and personal character, has the potential to become a leader. It demonstrates that everyone can be a change agent in a distinct way, without conforming to social norms. As an introvert like Carson, I prefer to live quietly, doing my work and simple everyday things that I enjoy. Amid the noise and chaos of the modern world, technology and social media have become the preferred tools for social good. We are also used to seeing change agents advocating their causes in groups or non-profit organizations. As a complement to these approaches, Carson's quiet leadership style is exceptionally

---

17 Koehn, Nancy, "From Calm Leadership, Lasting Change," *The New York Times*. October 27, 2012. http://www.nytimes.com/2012/10/28/business/rachel-carsons-lessons-50-years-after-silent-spring.html.

18 Sukel, Kayt, "The Legacy of SILENT SPRING: A Q&A with William Souder," Big Think. 2015. http://bigthink.com/world-in-mind/the-legacy-of-silent-spring-a-qa-with-william-souder.

19 Koehn, Nancy, "From Calm Leadership, Lasting Change," *The New York Times*. October 27, 2012. http://www.nytimes.com/2012/10/28/business/rachel-carsons-lessons-50-years-after-silent-spring.html.

refreshing. Learning about it made me stop and reflect. She did not set out to be a leader. She had no idea how influential *Silent Spring* would become or how great a change she would bring about. Yet today, she is regarded as a trailblazer, and rightfully so. As Professor Williams said during his session, one individual has the power to make a difference in the world, no matter how big or small.

There is so much one can learn from Carson's story. Behind her calm and quiet façade was a hardworking, persistent woman who fought through adversity to change the world. Carson's personal life was full of trials and tribulations, but she kept them private. She suffered a string of serious illnesses, including ulcers, pneumonia, and later breast cancer, all while having to care for her five-year-old grandnephew and her ailing mother.[20] Most people would have given up, but Carson remained relentless and managed to finish her book. When Carson went to testify before Congress, less than a year after *Silent Spring* was published, she had already survived a radical mastectomy; she was suffering from pelvis fractures that made it difficult for her to walk; and she was already dying of breast cancer.[21] Despite her frail condition, she mustered the strength to continue making public appearances in the last few years of her life because she believed that she could make a difference. From the first day of her journey, she understood the challenge but persevered because she wanted people to know the truth. She wrote to a friend, "There would be no future

---

20 Ibid.
21 Griswold, Eliza, "How 'Silent Spring' Ignited the Environmental Movement," *The New York Times Magazine.* September 21, 2012. http://www.nytimes.com/2012/09/23/magazine/how-silent-spring-ignited-the-environmental-movement.html.

peace for me if I kept silent."[22]

Nelson Mandela once said, "Education is the most powerful weapon which you can use to change the world." Carson's story proves how education can significantly influence people's mindsets and shape new perspectives, effects that can in turn be translated into actions to enact positive social change. Education also gives people a deeper sense of fulfillment and the authority to lead in challenging situations. In the face of strong criticism, Carson remained steadfast and was not worried about the consequences of writing *Silent Spring* because she knew that her book was based on hard facts and extensive research, including interviews with scientists, physicians, librarians, conservationists, and government officials.[23] Her sincerity, humility, strong will, and eagerness to absorb as much knowledge as possible made her a well-informed leader who carved a revolutionary path, stirring up the new generation to protect the world we live in.

Rachel Carson might not have lived to see the full impacts of her hard work, but more than fifty years after *Silent Spring* was first published, her courage still inspires individuals to demand change and question authority. During the ALE program, Mr. Kim told us that, to become effective leaders, we must know ourselves and build our own personal brands. He said that leaders need to know what they are doing, as they can only lead effectively when they feel strongly about their causes. Hence, we must be the best version of ourselves if we want to catalyze change. Rachel Carson enacted the change she

---

22 Koehn, Nancy, "From Calm Leadership, Lasting Change," *The New York Times*. October 27, 2012. http://www.nytimes.com/2012/10/28/business/rachel-carsons-lessons-50-years-after-silent-spring.html.

23 Ibid.

wanted to see in the world in her own way, on her own terms. In her case, it was change through the power of words—an inspiring demonstration that the pen is mightier than the sword.

Can a Butterfly in Argentina Cause a Tornado in China?

We live in a complex world that is becoming more and more interdependent. Now, more than ever, the demand for effective leaders is at an all-time high in order to address today's complicated challenges. During the ALE program, Professor Williams vividly described how every single thing that we do, no matter how small it is, in any part of the world, can have large and far-reaching ripple impacts elsewhere, through the "butterfly effect" concept. The concept implies that the simple flap of a butterfly's wing in a country like Argentina can affect complex systems, such as weather patterns which could set off a series of events that could cause a tornado halfway across the globe, like in China. In exercising leadership as change agents, Professor Williams encourages us to apply this concept to our daily lives by being aware of emerging global trends and recognizing the repercussions caused by the "butterfly effect" at the local level, in which they could pose new challenges as well as fascinating opportunities.

Professor Williams stresses the importance of making the right decision, as it has its own potential "butterfly effect," and hence we should never underestimate how it can influence people's lives on a larger scale than we ever imagined. So, if we think Trump's presidency won't affect us because we're not American, think again. In his first week in office, the new president issued executive orders that openly discriminate against minorities and bar refugees from entering the U.S., causing worldwide chaos and panic.[24] These are just warning signs of things to come as Americans and people from other countries wonder whether they will be safe in Trump's America. There have even been reports of Trump silencing government scientists with gag orders, putting politics above science.[25] Looking at the current situation, it appears that Trump is dragging America and the rest of the world backward.

Carpe Diem!

In order to thrive in times of uncertainty, Professor Williams advises us to never give up and easily swayed by other people's opinions. He urges us to have courage to disrupt the status quo, to stay focused on our purpose, and to let challenges fuel our passion to ignite lasting change in making the world a better place. Most importantly, we should seize opportunities amid hardships, and let them shape us as effective leaders.

Exercising leadership as a global change agent in this crazy and fractured world is not easy, as we may feel exhausted, emotionally drained, become skeptical about our abilities, and eventually burn out.[26] However, this is our opportunity to build our capacity for

---

24 Torbati, Yeganeh, et al., "Chaos, anger as Trump order halts some Muslim immigrants," *Reuters*. January 29, 2017. http://www.reuters.com/article/us-usa-trump-immigration-chaos-idUSKBN15C0LD.
25 Plait, Phil, "Make America Gagged Again," Slate.com. January 25, 2017. http://www.slate.com/blogs/bad_astronomy/2017/01/25/trump_issues_gag_orders_on_science_agencies.html.
26 Williams, Dean. *Leadership for a Fractured World*. Oakland: Berrett-Koehler

greater resilience in facing increasing challenges in life.[27] Professor Williams' advice on having the willingness to experiment and to move into unchartered territory regardless of the outcome struck a chord with me, as I do believe that we should at least try and give our best in whatever we do in life. So, if we feel that we are too insignificant to make an impact, take the first step and see where it leads you. Leadership itself is a journey of self-discovery that enables us to understand ourselves better and explore our potential to not only survive but to flourish, and to find enjoyment and fulfillment in shaping the future. Exploring a new frontier starts with imagination that unleashes a world of possibilities, fresh perspectives, and creative solutions to achieve our goals and create change.

Reflecting on the ALE program reminds me of an inspiring quote from one of my favorite movies, *Dead Poets Society*: "They're not that different from you, are they? Same haircuts. Full of hormones, just like you. Invincible, just like you feel. The world is their oyster. They believe they're destined for great things, just like many of you. Their eyes are full of hope, just like you. Did they wait until it was too late to make from their lives even one iota of what they were capable? Because you see gentlemen, these boys are now fertilizing daffodils. But if you listen real close, you can hear them whisper their legacy to you. Go on, lean in. Listen. Do you hear it? … Carpe … Hear it? Carpe. Carpe diem. Seize the day boys. Make your lives extraordinary."

So, you see, we all have the power to make a difference regardless of life's circumstances. The question is: What will you do with it?

Publishers, Inc, 2015.
27 Ibid.

| Chapter 9 |

A Bangladeshi Tale of Digital Dilemmas

Sheikh Mohammed Irfan

● ● ●

Introduction

When I was very young, my grandfather used to tell me that I would one day lead my country into greatness. "To lead the people, you must first understand them. And to understand them, you must know their history," he would say. Given to me by my grandfather, most of my childhood books and bedtime stories consisted of biographies of great leaders, narratives of the rise and fall of empires, and the history of nations. Reading about wars showed me the versatility, agility, and resilience of human nature. Learning of great leaders like Genghis Khan and Lee Kuan Yew led me to the realization that people need great leadership to fulfill their utmost potential. Surprisingly, the more I learned about history, the more I was able to identify my own place in its complex mesh of civilizations. Although he never proclaimed it, I believe my grandfather was aware that, through this knowledge, I would be able not only to understand but more importantly to identify with the people—and that is where true leadership lies.

A Brief History of Bangladesh

My journey, in essence, begins with the journey of my people. Bangladesh, known as the dazzling delta, has no shortage of resources, inspiration, or aspiration. In our forty-five-year history, we have battled with politics, hunger, poverty, education, and unemployment. Born from the ashes of three million lives during our war of independence with Pakistan, the people battled to create an infrastructure that remains the bulwark of our nationhood. Our history is sketchy and, in many ways, fabricated to impose certain ideologies on the country. I will here offer a brief history of the Bengal region, as it is crucial for us to understand our past in order to shape our future.

The region of Bangladesh was first denoted as "Banga" by the Proto-Dravidian Bong tribe that settled in the area circa 1,000 BCE. In this period, the region was a place of prosperity and trade; however, in time it was drawn into regional skirmishes with expansionist neighbors. Foreign cultures, politics, religions, and values were imposed on its people. Nevertheless, we demonstrated our own unique attributes. Trade, spiritual enlightenment, literature, and art were deep valued in the lives of the Bengali people. The region itself was a major influencer for these attributes; because it was so attractive, many different ethnic groups made the region their home and embodied the Bengali culture. Thus, the word "Bengali" indicates not so much a race as a lifestyle curated and demonstrated by the people living in Bengal.

Even today, people living in this region hold on to this regional identity and maintain these qualities as their national values. Sadly, other factors, such as religion, class, and political beliefs, have been used throughout history to define the region and promote "national consensus." This flawed "consensus" has always led to conflicts of interest and losses for the Bengali people. From the Hindu Kingdom in the early eras, followed by Buddhist rule, to Islamic Bengal and the colonialist period, our people have faced domination through laws, civic systems, and trade practices that marginalize non-religious affiliates. During the early era of colonial rule, the region battled famine. The colonialists introduced a foreign legal system, civic code, trade policy, and customs that eventually affected the entire region. Toward the end of colonial rule, a new pan-independence movement was introduced to create generality in the region.

The birth of "East Pakistan" in 1947 was the final nail in the coffin for the Bengali people. We were separated and classified according to our religious beliefs. During this time, a huge regional migration took place due to the artificial partition of West Bengal in India from "East Pakistan." This forced migration triggered a collapse of regional values. The new administration was further marginalized with the attempt to unite "East Pakistan" with "West Pakistan," causing a further disconnection with reality. It became increasingly apparent that the two regions, East and West, had little in common, and eventually the short-lived union came to a destructive end with the birth of Bangladesh in 1971.

Key Challenges Faced by Bangladesh

The new nation of Bangladesh faced numerous challenges, including the struggle to create a national identity. During the early years, all "East Pakistan" customs needed to be "cleansed" from society, but this was not easy, as many practices centered on the religion of Islam and the majority of people remained Muslim in Bangladesh. The state pronounced itself secular, yet maintained customs and code akin to the Muslim majority within the state, and this marginalized the country's huge group of non-Muslims. At the same time, Bengali nationalism was strong, owing to the victory and creation of the first Bengali nation since colonial times.

The nation was thus in a constant state of conflict, reinforced by differing political affiliations. This resulted in a still apparent fracture between the Islamic-oriented and culturally-oriented Bangladeshis. A "clan" differentiation also developed, due to years of local lordships carving out areas across the Bengal, thus further segregating the populace by introducing new values, social codes, and ethics. One may argue that this clan culture was an organic development arising locally from proximity and environment; however, deeper research reveals that these "lords" exerted a major influence on the nation as a whole. Today, their impact ranges from nepotism in workplaces to trade to personal relationships, and many fear that they pose a barrier to national growth.

Personal Leadership Challenges as a Bangladeshi

My journey thus began in the face of endless degeneration of my people's value system and code of ethics. I realized at an early age that I needed to function as a change agent, to lead my people back into the peace and prosperity that once unified us. The age of digitalization and Bangladesh's recent "Digital Bangladesh" initiative align perfectly with my goals. The power of technological innovation in mobilizing societies and facilitating change presents the perfect opportunity to transform the way we function as a society.

My initiative began when I encountered an organization called "Make It Happen." This organization aims to address the public's needs through direct technological interventions. At the time, they were working on solving the traffic issue within the metropolis of Dhaka, and they asked for my help in planning and implementing their project.

For over a decade, Dhaka city has been plagued with serious traffic issues due to overpopulation, unplanned urbanization, and the mismanagement of resources, among other things. Government authorities have tried to curb this problem for years with little success. "Make It Happen," however, managed to unite Dhaka's public over the frustrations they shared, using crowdfunding to support their initiative. Their plan was to create a traffic information application that would allow people to commute efficiently. The underlying philosophy of this project was in accordance with the theory of chaos: if a slight change in traffic conditions can create a major blockage, then the opposite is also true. This was a first-of-its-kind attempt within the country to create a product through crowdfunding. Almost immediately, ten thousand people backed the initiative and pledged their monetary commitment.

When I was approached to engineer this product, it resonated with me because of the cause and the story behind it. The project already had the financing, customer base, and technology needed to succeed, so I eagerly embarked on a two-month journey to develop the application. During this time, I was continuously in touch with the public, assessing their preferences and ensuring that my app would suit their needs. These interactions reinforced my belief that technology can bridge obstacles and unite people.

Finally, the big day arrived for the beta launch of our product. We were all confident with our product. We assumed that since our customers had backed us during every stage of development, our product was already customer-approved. But this assumption would cost us dearly. After the initial hype, during which our customers evangelized the app through social media, friend circles, etc., it became clear that we were facing a data crisis. Everyone wanted the convenience of knowing when and where to avoid traffic, but few wanted to go through the hassle of uploading that same information for public knowledge. Though willing to support the initiative monetarily, they were not ready to invest their time in it.

Although it was a shock, this experience taught me a valuable lesson about society's rigidity when it comes to changing the status quo. Traffic and congestion had become a way of life in Dhaka city, and people managed to plan their day around it. They soon decided that, regardless of the information provided by the traffic app, they would still be stuck in traffic, so they would rather do something enjoyable—read a book, eat a snack, chat, or take a nap—than upload information. Transforming old habits into new ones is easier said than done.

Another major assumption that we made while creating this app was that people would have alternative routes when commuting. In truth, Dhaka has only a couple of major routes, to which people are limited. Shortly after the launch, we realized that without direct collaboration from the authorities, we would not be able to change the traffic issues. Frustratingly, it soon became clear that if we had established relationships with all the players in traffic management (i.e. the government, the commuters, the transport providers, etc.), the result would have been quite different. Overall, the initiative taught me that while it is easy to start a reform, the same cannot be said about establishing and maintaining a new order. Many reforms start in a fever but fizzle out due to an inability to establish reliable replacements.

Despite these setbacks, we continued publicizing the app. Without a high frequency of data and reliable information, however, we were unable to keep our growing customer base content. Before we could resolve the issues at hand, our competitors started taking steps to leapfrog our initiative. Learning from our mistakes, they created a simpler and more successful product. They understood that, in order to succeed, their product must present a blend between innovation and tradition. Their product allowed users to access traffic information through both modern and traditional means. Rather than relying on the commuters themselves to update the traffic status of the roads, they hired employees to provide real-time data updates through the app. Soon, they were able to offer a constant flow of information to their customers.

Where our technologically advanced and skillfully engineered product had failed, our competitors' simple and practically designed product succeeded. We slowly lost our customer base as our competitors gained popularity. They were eventually able to establish themselves as the sole center of traffic information and, with a maximum customer base, received extensive funds to back their initiatives, while we continued bleeding. At this point, they incorporated all the niche features of our product within their system and managed to humble us completely. Before further damage could be done to our overall platform, our project was officially closed. Nevertheless, in the words of Henry Ford, "If everyone is moving forward together, then success follows." Although it did not turn out as originally planned, I believe we were still able to reach our goal of improving the problem of traffic in Dhaka city.

As Winston Churchill wisely put it, "Success is going from failure to failure with enthusiasm." Through my endeavors, I was able to gain recognition and establish myself as a powerful innovator with the ability to create disruptive technology. My efforts to become a change agent were bolstered by my peers, and the market identified me as a mover willing to take his chances. This gave me renewed confidence and helped me continue with my project to transform society. However, experience had taught me to become more cautious in my entrepreneurial approach. I knew now that innovation alone could not transform society, unless the people were willing and ready to adapt the change.

It was during this period of added publicity that I received a proposition directly threatening my principles. One day, I received a call from an enthusiastic customer, who had devised a plan for a new product. Naturally, the prospect of developing a new product is always attractive, but I maintained caution. I arranged to meet and discuss this prospective product with the organization in question. During our board-level meeting, thanks to my insistence on understanding the purpose of the product, it became apparent that it was designed to do something ethically vague—"neither legal nor illegal," as they tactfully put it. My first instinct was to report their activities to the authorities, but, as if predicting my response, they provided evidence that they were already working with the authorities. Despite their efforts to persuade me monetarily, I declined their proposal and asked them not to contact me or my company again. However, refusing such an organization turned out to be no easy task.

A week later, the organization approached me again, this time offering double their original payment. This process continued until their final offer was ten times the original value. When they realized that it would not be possible to convince me, they decided to try a different strategy: they began contacting some of my employees and trying to poach them. This created an uneasy environment within my organization, and I knew I needed to take decisive action. Swiftly, I announced a meeting in which I summoned every member of my organization. I laid the facts in front of my team members and allowed them to choose what they felt was right. I also underlined the philosophy behind my refusal to work with the other organization. I knew that by doing so, I risked losing some members of my team, but I felt that regardless of risk, I could not allow my organization to embrace a questionable ideology. Surprisingly, my transparency about my conduct received full appreciation from my staff, who all assured me that they agreed with my decision.

"Honesty is the single most important factor having a direct bearing on the final success of an individual, corporation, or product," said Ed McMaho. My decision to offer clarity on my actions reinforced my employees' morale and improved their overall performance. The experience taught me that when a large group of people possess all the facts, they will usually make the right decision. And even if the group fails to do so, it will at least be on the record that they were aware they had a choice.

Over time, I was able to expand my local projects and subsequently started looking for growth globally. Recently the financial market had showed signs of possible technological innovations, and in this area I thought I could make significant changes. After graduating from MIT's Fintech (Financial Technology) program in the School of Architecture and Design, I felt the time was right to step into the industry, on both a local and a global level. Hence, I embarked on a mission to give the public access to decentralized monetary processes, as well the power to decide on financial processes.

Effecting this transformation, of course, presented challenges. Banks had already established themselves as one of the oldest institutional service providers in Bangladesh, and they had a great understanding of the market, along with the reputation of being trusted middle-men. My first task was to enable blockchain technology for everyday functions. Blockchain is an open, distributed ledger that records transactions between two parties efficiently and in a verifiable and permanent way. The ledger itself can be programmed to trigger transactions automatically. By design, blockchains are resistant to modification—once recorded, the data in a block cannot be altered retroactively. This function and the fact that the entire system is secure opened up realms of opportunities.

I decided to begin by creating a virtual cluster in which people, regardless of their origins, could unite and build a community to script and shape the digital civilization; we called it the Global FinTech Village, and through it we gathered what had been a disjointed global movement into a single united force that we hoped would, among other things, ensure a transparent rewards system. Once this group was created, the next task seemed more attainable. We continued our process of knowledge transfer, aligning resources and furthering our education in the field of fintech.

Entering new territory entailed dealing skillfully with new players, concepts, regulations, and philosophies. Along with the challenge of bringing together a disjointed community, we needed to navigate the administrative restrictions set by different countries. I realized early on that it was important to work closely with financial institutions, governments, and consumers across the globe in order to turn our initiative into a success.

Eventually, we were able to incorporate our networking channels and identified key personnel in different fields who would champion our cause. The process was slow and took patience, but I knew that innovation, however radical it may be, must evolve organically rather than with brute force. My key takeaway from this experience was that, regardless of change in the external environment, true innovation develops internally.

Pathways to Becoming the Change Agent I Hope to Be

As I ventured into various worlds where I wanted to create change, I felt, despite all my efforts, that I was still inexperienced. In particular, I wanted to improve my leadership skills—both personally and socially. In spite of my passion and strengths, many of my past errors stemmed from my lack of skill in using different perspectives—both zooming in and zooming out, both short- and long-term—as well as in developing self-awareness, self-management, social awareness, and relationship management. In order to succeed on a larger scale, I needed to discover who I really was, where my place in this world was, and what work would provide the most important help to my country of Bangladesh and the world.

My luck turned when I met Mr. Hungsoo S. Kim in March 2016, during the Asia Innovation Trek, organized by CALI. The Trek was a socioeconomic study tour for scholars at Harvard University, who traveled to three cities—Seoul, Taipei, and Tokyo—to learn innovation and entrepreneurship in Asia and to network with Asian trend and thought leaders. Some months afterward, Mr. Kim led a program for leaders entitled, "Leading Change for Organizational Renewal." Since I was at a juncture where I needed both personal and professional reinvigoration, I enthusiastically joined this program. And as I embarked on my studies with Professor Dean Williams, my experiences proved more enlightening than I could have possibly imagined.

In the first few hours of the program, I started to gain a new understanding of the nature of leadership. Soon I was able to reflect on the choices I had made and how I could have made them better. Real leadership, as I learned, does not depend on what position, title, or authority you hold. It is about facing reality and making others face it, through interventions that create a new path or perspective. Crossing boundaries and understanding each side of a conflict while remaining vigilant, agile, and quick to respond are key to traversing the gray areas of life. Most importantly, the program enhanced my ability to appraise my own thoughts and actions, thus allowing me to progress and develop. It was transformational indeed, giving me an array of new ideas and ways to exercise and strengthen my leadership skills. In the past, I tended to resort to resources and aids external to myself. I would try to improve a system by laying out a better incentive structure, introducing new practices for my employees, and using my position to advance an agenda. Now, I first examine my situation from within, reflecting upon whether a way of addressing the challenges, problems, or opportunities ahead lies within me. I always assume that I may be the problem and that I may be the one who needs to change. I am now able to read between the lines and can work as a change agent with a deeper understanding of my role, which requires being prepared for anything and everything. We all face similar challenges, and recognizing this fact enables us to learn from and assist each other. All in all, this three-day program helped me to make another leap forward.

I also gained two additional key takeaways. First, people often blame their leaders, the government, or "others" for their problems. We rarely ask ourselves, "How are we as individuals contributing to or affecting our community?" Second, there is a misconception that one individual is too insignificant to create change. The fact is, however, that when individuals carry out initiatives on a micro level, the macro environment shifts through a ripple effect.

Institutional pillars are needed to support a grand structure, but no such pillars can take shape if the idea of the "institution" is not embedded in the individual. For example, recently, the Dhaka South City Corporation campaigned for a city cleaning drive. They installed approximately eight thousand trash bins across public areas. A few months later, it was reported that about six thousand of these bins had been stolen. The thefts raised the huge question of how individuals can be encouraged to take responsibility for their actions and to change their mindsets, in order to improve their lives and surroundings. It is important for us to take ownership of our actions and change ourselves before expecting the world around us to change.

As the wise Dalai Lama once said: "If you think you are too small to make a difference, try sleeping with a mosquito in the room." My experience has taught me the importance not only of knowing other people but of knowing myself. Humans seek knowledge instinctively, and we are born with a curiosity that blooms with our mastery of expression, when we are able to use language to question everything from our own existence to the laws of nature. "Sapere aude," or "dare to know," is the motto I live by, and every day is an adventure in which I explore the boundless sea of knowledge presented by the universe. In the end, I know that the best path to success lies in being kind. And I am excited to see what the next five, ten, and even thirty years of my life will bring, as I strive to be a linchpin of my community's success.

| Chapter 10 |

A Muslim Woman's Success and Failures in Leadership

Shamza Khan

● ● ●

> *Plain speech matters because when we speak clearly, we are more likely to speak truth than when we retreat into euphemism. Avoiding euphemism takes courage because it almost always points plainly to responsibility.*
>
> — *Adam Gopnik, New Yorker*

A Road Less Traveled: Growing Up in Hong Kong

Growing up as a Pakistani girl in Hong Kong's capitalist society was a definitive and dramatic experience. Ethnically, I'm from a highly emotional, religious, poor, rich, beautiful, derelict, passionate, corrupt, developing, and dysfunctional country—Pakistan. Leaders in Pakistan have a high tendency for corruption, but they can also be charming, opinionated, and influential. Being raised in a highly linear, law-abiding, professionally driven, global financial hub—Hong Kong—was an extreme contrast to Pakistani culture. Leaders in Hong Kong are typically systematic, strategic, transparent, and honest. I grew up therefore, in a collision of two opposite worlds, two distinctly different cultures.

My father's generation in Hong Kong did well because the British leadership in Hong Kong had established transparent rules for career success: learn Cantonese, follow the rules, and remain loyal to the British system. My father arrived in Hong Kong from Pakistan in 1958 and said one thing to himself: "I'm never going back, without succeeding here." Eventually, he became a senior police officer and was rewarded with a secure job and significant government benefits as a British civil servant. It was a huge accomplishment for the sixteen-year-old Pakistani youth who had left his village in Punjab seeking a better life.

My own experience in Hong Kong was far more certain because of the tremendous head start that my father gave me. Still, there was no established path for Pakistanis in Hong Kong in the 1960s and '70s, when my brothers and I were born, despite the fact that Pakistani migrants to Britain and America had affected the social-political discourse in those countries. My brothers and I were among the first generation of Pakistanis in Hong Kong belonging to a professional working family. We attended prestigious British schools, which cut us off from Hong Kong's mainstream Chinese society. At the same time, my parents taught us to respect our host country and its people, to show allegiance to the British Queen, and to be honest and professional in our work.

For a first-world country, Hong Kong has been exceptionally slow in developing forward-looking race relations. In the 1970s, the Hong Kong Cantonese gravitated toward an extreme negative bias regarding ethnic minorities; frankly speaking, they were racist. I knew that as a Pakistani I had to dress better, speak better, know better, and present myself better than anyone else, in order to avoid hostility. For this, however, I am extremely grateful—Hong Kong made me work hard at building relationships and creating networks; it pushed me to excel. My experience was different from my father's because he was a police officer within the British government—his position commanded respect, and the people who worked for him and with him were forced to respond to his authority. My situation, in contrast, was muddled: I had to navigate between a posh, discriminating British school and the prejudice from Hong Kong Cantonese on the streets.

Nevertheless, Hong Kong did many things well. Being a woman in Hong Kong was a non-issue; I can honestly say I have never experienced gender bias there. In Pakistan, which ranks 122nd out of 125 on the gender gap index, I had the opposite experience. Having spent every childhood summer in my parents' village in Punjab, I know firsthand how difficult it is to be a girl in Pakistan. Every aspect of our lives was scrutinized and controlled: what we wore, how we spoke, whom we spoke to. We were never allowed to interact with boys. At times in Punjab, I felt that I alone was responsible for my whole family's respect and honor—a strict code rooted in religion but also based on the traditions of a close family, aunties, uncles, and society at large. The extreme restraints led to a constant tension between my own sense of self and the cultural, ritual, and religious observances imposed by our families on us girls.

Given Pakistan's deeply rooted Muslim culture and my family's adherence to it, it is not surprising that, despite Hong Kong's capitalist and agnostic society, I had to obey many Muslim and Pakistani conventions there too. I was not allowed to talk to boys on the phone, to wear skirts or dresses, to attend sex education classes, or to attend swimming classes comfortably. I had to take Quran lessons, and Friday prayers at the mosque were compulsory. My mother constantly warned me to preserve my Muslim identity at all costs. These restraints were often frustrating, but there are also many elements of my Pakistani and Muslim heritage that I value. I'm grateful to come from a tradition of overwhelming love and support, and I'm also cognizant of the fact that my parents struggled with having a nonconventional daughter like me, who not only challenged their rituals, religion, and cultural norms but also confronted them about many of their core beliefs. The reason I consider my parents to be exceptional is that, at the end of the day, they still love me deeply and genuinely. I feel blessed because their love for me is unconditional, and that is not the norm for girls in Pakistan.

Having adapted to both Hong Kong and Pakistan's extremes, I understand that there are tremendous advantages to being raised in a first-world country with many inherent freedoms, and that there is magic in being Pakistani. The British colonial heritage, which both Pakistan and Hong Kong possess, ties my complex package neatly together. Having British citizenship and being a Hong Kong resident, with a big dose of Pakistani traditions, has ultimately given me huge advantages in life—and set me on a contrarian path.

Leadership 101: Know Thyself (The New York Magic)

Without self-awareness, you can't know your strengths, weaknesses, your "super–powers" vs. your "kryptonite"...
— Anthony K. Tjan, Harvard Business Review

Mr. Hungsoo S. Kim emphasized the importance of self-awareness in his opening address to the ALE program. Confirming that self-awareness lies at the heart of being a good leader, he talked about his personal journey, about not only confronting but actively engaging in the challenges he faced and how he dealt with them. When you meet authentic leaders, no matter what their position in society, they seem relatable, trustworthy, and open; one feels connected to their journeys. I felt the same way listening to Mr. Kim: his message was genuine, heartfelt, and real. His talk set the tone for everything else in the class, and it held a lot of significance for me. One simple framework in his guide to self-awareness was the following:

- Being—*Heart*
- Knowing—*Head*
- Doing—*Hands*

Our heart enables us to understand who we are; our head focuses on knowledge acquisition and information; and our hands are the tools we use to drive change, practicing what we know to make a positive contribution in the world. Both Mr. Kim and Professor Dean Williams wove stories of their own experiences into their classes and projected their own confidence. They encouraged all of us to contribute, express ourselves, and share stories about our leadership journeys.

In my own journey, two pivotal factors drove my self-discovery process. One was fighting constraints in my upbringing that I thought were unfair—biases and barriers that felt either hypocritical or irrational, such as not being allowed to attend mixed gatherings without my parents or brothers, to move away from home, to continue my studies, and to travel freely for work or pleasure. I did not have any female mentors growing up. My mother is an opinionated Muslim woman whom I love deeply, and my grandmother was a strong woman who commanded a lot of respect—but I viewed them both as religiously and culturally entrenched. Only later was I lucky enough to be coached, challenged, and supported by two female mentors who made a huge impact on me.

The second key factor in my self-awareness journey was my love for travel, meeting different people, and experiencing new worlds. These inclinations led me to live and work in places across Asia, Europe, and the U.S. My broad and deep cross-cultural experiences have helped me understand the nuances of many countries, regions, and peoples, and they have also exposed me to surprising biases. For example, I was shocked to find out that many Jewish women in New Jersey and New York face tremendous pressure to get married in their early twenties. Initially this seemed strange to me, but it also taught me that no matter what our upbringing or faith, fundamental biases and beliefs transcend boundaries too.

When I arrived in the U.S. for the first time in 1998—to meet Enron Corporation's CEO, Jeff Skilling, for an interview in New York City—I was expecting a magical American grandness, the kind we had grown up seeing in movies, eating in their food, moonwalking to in "Billie Jean," and essentially spending our whole lives trying to experience. Instead, JFK Airport felt like a multiracial version of the Karachi airport in Pakistan. It was extremely discouraging at first, but when I started living in New York, I discovered that its gifts lie under the surface. Its ultimate gift is total freedom: once there, I was able to drop all constraints and discover who I really was. New York was where I explored the full meaning and weight of my Muslim heritage, my Pakistani roots, and my Hong Kong origins. The city gave me the space and mental bandwidth not only to reflect on who I was but also to design a value system that belongs to me alone, without any external pressures or influences. In forming this system, I let go of many unnecessary burdens and expunged what I felt was religious, cultural, and ritualistic clutter.

I am grateful for my work as a professional writer because it takes me to new places like New York. It gives me the freedom to navigate through gray areas, to jump into situations that are moral minefields, and to connect with other people's dreams and sorrows. I may not be a great writer, but I write honestly. Ultimately, this achievement is the source of my self-worth.

Leadership in Practice: Success and Failure

Perfect oases don't exist in this world—not in countries, organizations, teams, or relationships—because all choices involve trade-offs. Dealing with extreme cultural contrasts has enabled me to develop skills in working through the world's complexity. As I gained experience as a business and academic writer, I realized that my emotions played a key role in my analytical thinking—they helped me process organizational and cultural complexity.

What Professor Williams and Mr. Kim reinforced during our executive education class was that leaders today face massive, multidimensional problems. No one person or group can possibly solve them; they require the broadest possible cooperation. But our leadership models are still essentially tribal: individuals with formal authority, leading in the interest of their own groups. We need leadership that transcends boundaries, whether those boundaries are cultural, organizational, political, geographic, religious, or structural. Sometimes leaders themselves have to be the ones who cross the boundaries. Other times, a leader's job is to build bridges between divided groups or even to break down the boundaries that block collaborative problem solving. By thinking about power and authority in a different way, leaders can become genuine change agents, able to heal wounds, resolve conflicts, and bring a fractured world together.

In 2007, I was living in Islamabad and working for USAID, the global development agency under the U.S. State Department. In two years of living in Pakistan as an adult and a mother, I had seen the tremendous negative impact of capitalism, corruption, and dysfunctional markets, which put many families and children in a perpetual poverty trap. What I saw had changed my views on Hong Kong's and New York's capitalist systems and outcomes. Then the U.S. government announced its pledge to give Pakistan $5 billion in foreign assistance, and at the same time I got to know Amy Meyer, a young, passionate, committed American woman also working for USAID. Amy inspired me to think about the contributions I could make in Pakistan's private sector, given my advantages as an American-educated Pakistani. She talked about making a transformational impact on Pakistan. Her vision was to create six hundred thousand direct jobs, transform twenty thousand small and medium-sized enterprises (SMEs), increase Pakistan's overall trade by 5 percent, and help eighty thousand female micro-entrepreneurs. It seemed impossible to say no to her. This was my calling.

Amy handpicked eight women to be on her leadership team for the $500 million Economic Growth portfolio for USAID in Pakistan. Her approach was ambitious and at times controversial, but her dogmatic commitment to maximizing results for Pakistanis seemed like exactly what was needed to deliver substantive results. She insisted on setting an example through her own actions—one of her main aims was giving opportunities to women, and the other was implementing best practices and designing projects with the best possible outcomes for Pakistanis. Together we defied the default practice of hiring men and pushed the boundaries of USAID's bureaucracy, Pakistan's government, and the contractors we hired. It was an uphill battle, but we were strong in our like-minded determination.

You could say we were what Professor Williams called "earth shakers"—pursuing our vision but more importantly stirring people into action and convincing them to face reality. We had $500 million for our Economic Growth team alone, and we knew we had a unique opportunity to do something powerful. Instead of thinking in terms of projects, we began to ask ourselves, "How can we fix Pakistan's entire private sector with our funds?" As Mr. Kim later outlined in his course, our team attempted to cross inter-organizational boundaries and overcome communication barriers with local partners, including the government and private sector players, so that we could buck the trend of typical projects, reduce the money spent on contractors, and increase the resources filtering through to Pakistani firms, entrepreneurs, and the private sector. Within USAID and the State Department, we spoke up, trying to change the rules of the game where we could; to develop innovative solutions, such as collective signatures on procurement documents; and to advocate our ideas on education, health, and economic growth. We felt confident that our strategy was the right approach to meet both U.S. and Pakistani objectives.

Our shared vision was extremely empowering. Amy supported our innovations, and we named our entire range of private sector projects "Empower Pakistan." Contractors and implementing partners typically don't work well together, but we made it a condition that contractors and sub-contractors operate in the same office space and come up with integrated goals instead of working within their own narrow objectives. Championing change was an exhilarating and unique experience. We practiced deep breathing before every meeting, conducted our meetings under trees in open gardens, brainstormed at spiritual shrines, prayed, fed the poor, and met Pakistani men and women from all over the country. In leadership terms, I would say we practiced both the spiritual and the technical quotients.

Now, did all of these efforts, began with such great intentions, go well? No. The project did not create the impact we had envisioned and worked so hard to achieve. What happened? The program with Professor Williams and Mr. Kim gave me a chance to look back and muse over why our project unfolded so differently from the way we had intended.

At an organizational level, we were unable to break down silos and build the inter-departmental bridges critical for meeting our integrated objectives. Different departments within USAID—Health, Education, Agriculture, and Economic Growth—had competing priorities. We were also affected by the State Department waging a "war on terror" in Pakistan, which not only created a lot of suspicion and mystery in our workplace but also led to an extremely cautious approach to our projects. An internal joke was "You will be punished for doing the right thing!" Further breakdowns occurred because senior USAID leadership constantly changed and the State Department's goalposts kept shifting. While the Economic Growth team did engage in straight talk with the contractors and other Pakistani stakeholders, I don't believe we gave an adequate answer to their question, "What is the breakthrough?" In retrospect, despite our best efforts as a team, I think the overall organization focused too exclusively on the technical aspects of the project, such as reporting requirements, log frames, and Mission goals. Our team might have succeeded in framing our aspirations for Pakistan's economic growth, but ultimately we were hugely constrained by the USAID/State Department bureaucracy.

In an excellent article entitled "The Leader's Compass: Principles of Leadership to Generate Progress," Professor Williams talks about the challenge of producing progress. What most resonated with me were the following points:

- "Generating progress requires examining the prevailing assumptions, hidden in the background of key human pursuits." Our Economic Growth team's approach was to maximize Pakistan's private sector, supporting talented entrepreneurs across Pakistan's twenty fastest-growing districts with populations of twenty to thirty million. However, the decision to spend money through the Pakistani government infrastructure hampered our efforts significantly.

- "What is needed is a new kind of leadership that mobilizes people to face defects and deficiencies in their current systems, models, and modus operandi, so that progress can occur." USAID conducts studies on issues constraining its global development performance. However, in Pakistan, the USAID Mission either did not or could not mobilize the lessons these studies offered into actionable change. In addition, I did not feel that the Mission in Pakistan was really open to feedback; instead, organizational politics reigned supreme.
- "The uttermost essence of trust building and credibility." Since our stakeholders did not view USAID as an organization that "walked the talk," there was a great deal of real and perceived variance between our stated plans and the standards by which our counterparts played. More communication could have helped to build trust.
- Ultimately, there was plenty of "counterfeit leadership" in Pakistan's government organizations, as in many other governments. In Professor Williams' words, there was "an excessive focus and dependence on authority, hierarchy, prominence, and dominance." Our success was highly dependent on solving interlocking problems, and all the complexities we encountered highlighted that the old style and structure of leadership was no nearer to dealing

with the nation's problems.

Truth and Leadership: A Gritty Street

Despite the failure of our USAID project, I still believe in Mr. Kim's conviction that powerful ideas and strong guiding expertise can bring meaningful change to societies. I undertook a transformational leadership journey through my USAID work. Attending Mr. Kim's program five years after the project, I was struck by one point especially—that before we talk about changing systems and people, we need to look to ourselves and "walk the talk" in our own lives. One way to do this is to be both critical and compassionate toward one's own life. As a writer who focuses on how leaders and organizations rise and fall, I have witnessed the importance of such self-awareness in the lives of many leaders, as well as in myself.

Maybe the goddess Krishnamurti was wrong in saying that "truth is a pathless land." For people like me, disconnected from institutional doctrines, truth and leadership may form a gritty street with no signposts, but that doesn't mean we're lost; we're on a path too. In a world with weak leaders and pervasive injustice, it is still possible to retain our core values. We need to be leaders who fight from within ourselves and lead individuals at different levels. We must strive to be the best versions of ourselves in order to help and inspire those around us. When we face weak ethics, ineffective leadership, and negative cultures, we need to ask ourselves, "How can we move forward amidst dysfunctionality?"

Let me share with you what I've learned. The USAID Pakistan project was large, idealistic, and visionary, but it failed. However, we still managed to effect some change, and I'm proud of our endeavors. I learned from the experience that exercising leadership should begin with small things. Creating impact within my own individual sphere of influence is a worthwhile aim and one that I'm constantly striving to meet. For over fifteen years, I have been helping to support marginalized girls in Punjab. I engaged in this effort in order to work with the great women heroes of Pakistan and because I believe that my country still has a future. After all, Pakistan was the first Muslim country to elect a female Prime Minister—Benazir Bhutto in 1988. In 2012, the Speaker of the National Assembly, the Foreign Minister, the Information Minister, the Ambassador to the U.S., and the Acting Defense Secretary were all women. Sharmeen Obaid-Chinoy was Pakistan's first Oscar winner and continues to make headlines with her amazing stories. Over 22 percent of the lower house of Pakistan's Parliament and over 16 percent of the upper house are women—a higher percentage than one can find in India, the U.K., or the U.S. In Pakistan's public universities, female enrollment is much higher than male enrollment. Pakistani women play a major role in agricultural production, the care of livestock, and cottage industries; the last agricultural census stated that 73 percent of women participate in agriculture.

My overarching point is that seeking out those in need for a cause you support, is a useful and gratifying first step. In my work relationships, my basic aim is always to build trust and share knowledge. In my personal relationships, I try to positively influence everyone in my circle—my family, my friends, their families, my staff, their families, my team, their kids. Every day, I try to make realistic decisions that attend to my own interests but are not confined to them.

You may ask, "In a world where fame and grand gestures are valued so highly, what can one do as a quiet, everyday person?" For an answer, I suggest looking to Albert Schweitzer, a German man who gave up a promising career as a musician and theologian to work as a doctor among the poor in Central Africa. When he won the Nobel Peace Prize in 1952, Schweitzer used the prize money to build a facility for treating leprosy. He changed many lives and inspired countless others. In his autobiography, *Out of My Life and Thought*, he wrote these words: "Of all the will toward the ideal in mankind, only a small part can manifest itself in public action. All the rest of this force must be content with small and obscure deeds. The sum of these, however, is a thousand times stronger than the acts of those who receive wide public recognition. The latter, compared to the former, are like the foam on the waves of a deep ocean."[28]

---

28 Schweitzer, Albert. *Out of My Life and Thought.* New American Library (1963), 74.

| Chapter 11 |

Making This World a Better Place Through "Knowing, Doing, and Being"

Katherine Kee

● ● ●

Public relations (PR) is the strategic communication process that builds mutually beneficial relationships between organizations and their publics. The role of someone working in PR is mainly to provide news or information on the company to internal and external audiences, via unpaid or earned methods, through traditional media. One might think that this is an easy job, but it's not.

Being in PR is no easy feat. One has to be good at persuasion, storytelling, building relationships, and getting the right information. Friendly, outgoing, talkative, charming, a people's person—these terms describe an extrovert, and they apply also to the ideal of a PR practitioner, who needs to be an effective communicator.

Yet, strangely enough, this description does not describe me as a PR practitioner. I engage with a lot of people within the organization—people and students from diverse nationalities, backgrounds, and cultures. If I were an extrovert, this would probably be the most enjoyable part of my work. However, because I am an introvert, it takes me a while to build relationships with the people I work with.

In my line of work, going beyond my boundaries is routine. In fact, I had to do this recently at one of the networking events of the A-Levels program, a U.K. post-secondary program, which I attended so that I could write an article on it. I have to connect with those I come into contact with so that they will provide me with the information I need to write their story and document their experience. To make a connection, I usually look for common ground. Music, books, art, sports, or even a pet are great topics to begin the conversation. Without an ice-breaker of this kind, it can be difficult to generate a productive conservation. Fortunately, this is where my introversion helps: I have cultivated a good grasp of general knowledge on a wide range of subjects through the books I read, the research I do on the internet, and my understanding of the current news. This wealth of knowledge, I find, is very important to get my work started.

Starting the conversation is relatively easy. What I find more difficult is asking the right questions. While some people are willing to talk and share information, some are not. How do I get them to open up? When I complete the interview and sit down to write the articles, I have to think of the interviewees' purpose in telling me their stories and at the same time think about protecting their privacy. Being an introvert, I hate oversharing, so when I write the articles, I instinctively locate the balance between maintaining privacy and keeping my readers interested. Of course, one must also always be true to the intentions of the interviewee.

My favorite part of being a PR practitioner is the writing. When I sit down to write, I often need to find a quiet space and dig deep into my thoughts to start the process. This is my happiest time. My introverted nature has led me to believe in keeping my head down, doing the work, and letting it speak for itself. In many ways, this philosophy has served me well through the years, but I know I can do better.

> *"Don't underestimate the power of your vision to change the world. Whether that world is your office, your community, an industry or a global movement, you need to have a core belief that what you contribute can fundamentally change the paradigm or way of thinking about problems."*
> — *Leroy Hood, American biologist*

A year-long program at the Harvard Kennedy School of Government called "Adaptive Leadership"—an intense and powerful experience—was compressed into a three-day workshop for close to fifty of us in October 2016. One key takeaway from this program was that helping to make the world a better place begins with the power of one. Contributing to society requires just one individual, a leader who uses his or her power to be a voice for the voiceless.

In our world today, the fame and influence of celebrities like Angelina Jolie and Emma Watson have increased public awareness of humanitarian issues and the need to help those who are less fortunate. A Goodwill Ambassador from 2001-2012 for the United Nations High Commissioner for Refugees (UNHCR), Angelina Jolie has worked tirelessly to champion conservation, education, women's rights, and advocacy for refugees. As a Special Envoy in 2012, she carried out field missions that gave the world a clearer picture of the displacement crises faced by so many refugees. Emma Watson, made famous by her role as Hermione Granger in the Harry Potter film series, leveraged her fame to promote education for girls. Appointed as Goodwill Ambassador in 2014 by UN Women, the United Nations Entity for Gender Equality and the Empowerment of Women, Watson launched the UN Women campaign "HeForShe," an initiative engaging men in the fight for gender equality for the advancement of women. She said, "I invite you to step forward, to be seen, and to ask yourself, 'If not me, who? If not now, when?'"

Many of us feel that we are not famous or important. We are too busy and stressed out by the cares of our own lives to worry about helping others. We ask ourselves, "Why do something when no one will notice or know?" Perhaps we think that we will help when we have the time. According to Stephanie Watson, Executive Editor of the Harvard Women's *Health Watch*, volunteering may be good for the body and mind; studies have shown that volunteers have better mental and physical health. Doing good promotes happiness, and, according to Henry David Thoreau, "Goodness is the only investment that never fails."

This quotation was shared by Mr. Hungsoo S. Kim. He introduced three components that determine happiness. Fifty percent comes from what is called the set point. Simply put, your level of happiness is partly determined by your background—your parents, their professions, their income level, the house you grew up in, etc. These conditions were pre-determined, and you have no power over them. Meanwhile, 10 percent comes from your life's circumstances: the level and type of education you've received, your teachers, your friends, your employment and marital status, your income, etc. Again, these are not always factors you can determine. The last 40 percent, however, lies in intentional activities, the practices you choose to engage in. This means deciding how your life will look, including both cognitive and behavioral elements. It requires adopting a positive attitude, being kind to others, engaging in physical exercise, setting and striving toward goals, etc. What I learned from Mr. Kim's talk is that there is a great deal of things we can do to make our lives more meaningful and worthwhile. Lending a helping hand to others, be it small or significant, will add value to both other people's lives and ours, making our world a better place to live in.

The session led me to reflect on myself and the work I was doing. What can I do to make myself a contributing member of society, so that I can add value to the community I love? My reflection resulted in several questions: Do I consider my work a job, a career, or a calling? And what are my mid- to long-term intentions when it comes to my work? My reflection is still a work in progress, but Mr. Kim helped me to see the importance of linking my occupation to my identity. Rather than seeing my work as a pathway to achievement and prestige, I have started searching for possible positive effects that my current work can generate.

Mr. Kim also spoke of "knowing, doing, and being." He related the importance of understanding yourself—your key strengths, passions, and weaknesses, your role in leadership, knowing when and how to lead, and when and how to let others exercise leadership, and understanding how your contribution enhances the overall well-being of our society. The same themes were evident in Professor Dean Williams' later sessions on global change agents, in which he encouraged us all to be leaders who contribute to making the world a better place.

Such leadership is essential in today's world, whereby many are looking inward, becoming selfish and arrogant, and not caring about others, whether they are family, friends, or colleagues. Many people's idea of success entails moving quickly up the corporate ladder, making more money, retiring early, and only focusing on how to attain their individual goals, without thinking how it might impact others.

But success, I believe, is relative. People from different backgrounds measure success differently. For some, it means an honest job with enough to eat and a place to call home. For some, it means a high-flying job with a six-figure salary, a mansion, and the luxury to hop on a private jet at any time. For others, success means a stable job that pays enough to put decent food on the table, a roof over their heads, and a bit to be set aside for rainy days, with time and resources to help others who are less fortunate. It gladdens my heart that though they are few, this group chooses to help out and contribute to the communities they live in.

Years ago, I had the opportunity to help out at one of the soup kitchens in the city center. The soup kitchen provides a hot lunch every Saturday in a back alley, come rain or shine. There weren't many regular volunteers; most just dropped by once or twice and were never to be seen again. The idea of spending Saturdays dishing out food to the homeless in a dirty alley under the sweltering sun may not sound appealing, but the few who do so can be seen working diligently side by side. The canopy goes up, the tables are prepped, the pots of food are placed, and the work begins: dishing out food and serving drinks to the group of people who come every week. Many who gather for the meal are not homeless; they just do not have enough. Others come for the companionship. These precious few hours offer a time to catch up on the latest news, to escape temporarily the cares of the world, and to enjoy the camaraderie of being with those who care. Then reality sets in, when lunch is finished and the work of cleaning up begins.

As people become ever more materialistic and the economy takes a turn for the worse, I have worried in the past that many people will turn away from sharing or even caring. However, I now know that the power of just one leader can create powerful change.

When I first joined the Sunway Education Group (SEG) three years ago, I did not realize the vast amount of time and money that Dr. Jeffrey Cheah, Founder and Chairman of Sunway Group, has contributed to society. A man with a vision, a global change agent in his own right, he believes in the power of knowledge and education. To promote learning, he set up the Jeffrey Cheah Foundation, which over the years has provided countless opportunities for young people to continue their education through scholarships at SEG institutions. Sustainability and environmental protection are also important to him. Not only has he turned his disused tin mine into an integrated township, decorated with hospitals, malls, homes, and educational institutions, he also set up the Jeffrey Sachs Center on Sustainable Development in Malaysia to promote research and training in environmental sustainability. This Center aims to educate and inspire more people to step up, protect, and preserve the planet. Dr. Cheah is one who certainly practices "knowing, doing, and being."

Because of his efforts on behalf of the environment, I am happily doing my own bit to preserve the planet. To minimize the daily waste of resources, I print in black and white on both sides of paper, clear my own food trays, use glass drinking bottles, drink coffee grown by sustainable communities, and, in many other little ways, try to live a life of "knowing, doing, and being."

On the other side of the world, in the United States of America, former President Barack Obama tried his very best to do more before he left the Oval Office. According to a *Huffington Post* article dated November 25, 2016, former President Obama caused the Department of the Interior to ban gold mining on the doorstep of the Yellowstone National Park, cancelled thirty-two thousand acres' worth of mining leases in Montana, banned offshore drilling for five years in the Arctic, and carried out countless other measures to protect the environment. The Paris Agreement, the Clean Power Plan, and the world's largest marine reserve were all part of his contribution to saving the planet. Former President Obama is another prominent figure who practices "knowing, doing, and being."

With leaders who inspire us, we too should aim to contribute. Other people may not consider someone like me a leader, but that is not true. Their understanding of leadership requires a leader to be in a position of authority. However, after these three days of intensive learning, I know that I too can be a leader by mobilizing the people around me to address one of the many challenges that we all face. Through these small efforts, our actions become stones dropped in a pond, creating ripples that will eventually affect other people; their actions will in turn affect others, and the ripples will spread ever wider.

Ultimately, we need to aim to be more than just leaders; we need to become global change agents. As explained by Professor Williams, people who take up leadership roles need to stand firm and cross borders, inspiring people to generate change. Let us all start by doing our small bit, let us lead others by example. This thought leads me to another point, another noteworthy lesson from Professor Williams. Through the video he showed us entitled *Rides and Tides*, featuring Andy Goldsworthy, I learned about an artist who works with nature. The video impressed upon me the need for a leader who thinks like an artist: innovative, bold, and creative. One of the most important things about Goldsworthy's work is that the artist always uses his bare hands, not wearing gloves even when he works with snow and ice in the winter, because he needs to feel, touch, and sense his material when he is creating a piece of work.

My first exposure to good leadership came when I started working in a Japanese retail company after high school. Our directors and the general manager of the store often came to help when the queues at the cashier counters got too long. They lent helping hands, so that clerks, executives, supervisors, and managers all worked side by side. They took the time to greet each and every customer, leading by example and teaching us the importance of customer service. Many of us before then had not adhered to this principle, when the queues were long and we were tired out at the end of the day. Yet, the directors and the general manager put into practice what they preached, and in time all of us began to follow suit, greeting the customers enthusiastically and placing customer service as a top priority. In the end, we Malaysians learned to embrace a new norm.

Interestingly, Professor Williams also taught us the traits of counterfeit leaders, who focus on prominence and dominance. These counterfeit leaders tend to be talkative and expressive, to tell good stories (also known as kissing the Blarney Stone), and to give the rosiest version of the facts, offering what they believe the management would like to hear. According to Professor Williams, studies have shown that these people are dangerous for companies; they tend to push the organization into a downward spiral toward mediocrity or worse, collapse.

Real leaders are hard to find and change agents are even harder to locate. We do indeed live in a fractured world. The troubled state of countries around the world, the existence of corrupt leaders, people in power committing daylight robbery and oppressing the masses, the lack of great leaders who inspire—all of these disheartening factors have resulted in a downward spiral in the world's overall quality of life.

Nevertheless, I am happy to be where I am now, in my workplace. I am blessed to be surrounded by people who inspire me. As Brian Tracy, Chairman and CEO of Brian Tracy International, once said, "Become the kind of leader that people would follow voluntarily, even if you had no title or position." My colleagues help me to grow and see the person I should become as a leader in my work.

I believe that every one of us can be an agent of change; it just needs a bit of work and some tweaks along the way. Learning to be less selfish and more aware of the world around me, I also learned that there is hope for us yet. In the words of Joel A. Barker, the first person to popularize the concept of paradigm shifts, "Vision without action is merely a dream. Action without vision just passes the time. Vision with action can change the world."

| Editor's Acknowledgments |

● ● ●

On behalf of the Asia Leadership Institute (ALI), I wish to acknowledge everyone who contributed to the success of the three Asia Leadership Executive (ALE) programs, namely "Personal Leadership: Ethics, Power, and Decision Making," "Case Method Teaching: A Way Forward for Effective Pedagogy," and "Leading Change for Organizational Renewal," as well as the publication of this book. This book would not have become a reality without their help and support.

First and foremost, I would like to thank each of the authors for devoting their time and effort toward this book—Dr. Gin Chee Tong, Dr. Hendry Ng, Dr. Cordelia Mason, Yasmin M. Handrich, Elma Berisha, Peter K.H. Law, Ida Fazila Ismail, Sheikh Mohammed Irfan, Shamza Khan, and Katherine Kee.

Second, the Harvard Professors, namely Professor Kenneth Winston, Professor Mathias Risse, and Professor Dean Williams who graciously shared their knowledge, time, and invaluable insights with the participants. It was a great privilege to be able to learn from them and I am truly humbled by their dedication, effort, and generosity.

To the Teaching Fellows who exemplified passion and commitment to knowledge and excellence–Ms. Lisa Lee, Ed.M., Harvard Graduate School of Education (HGSE); Mr. Randy Tarnowski, Ed.M., HGSE; Mr. Panche Kralev, MCMPA, Harvard Kennedy School of Government (HKSG); Mr. John Lim, MALD, Fletcher School of Law and Diplomacy; and Ms. Wan Fong Woo, Ed.M., HGSE. I am grateful to have had the opportunity to work with such a talented, enthusiastic, and inspiring group of people.

To the Student Leaders who contributed their time and energy to ensure the smooth running of the programs—Ahmad Aniq bin Mohd Nooramin Kaw, Ang Wei Boon, Chan Choon Hee, Wong Li Min, Wong Shen Ni, Yoon Peili, Ashley Tan Huey Lin, Avryl Ooi Wan Cheen, Chan Mei Yen, Chow Shenn Kuan, Darshini Rani Bissoondeeal, Jannice Tan Wei Chee, Mohammad Shakirin bin Shahrul Jamal, Thinesh Naidu Nagiah, and Serena Kaan Tsu Li.

I deeply appreciate the hard work and active participation of the Organizing Committee whose tremendous support contributed to the successful organization of the programs—Tan Zhi Kai, Ryan Lee Juin Jie, Shannon D. Francis, Gan Shan Xin, Yeoh Guan Aik, and Serena Kaan Tsu Li for the "Personal Leadership: Ethics, Power, and Decision Making;" and "Case Method Teaching: A Way Forward for Effective Pedagogy" programs, as well as Mohammad Shakirin bin Shahrul Jamal, Ang Wei Boon, and Serena Kaan Tsu Li for the "Leading Change for Organizational Renewal" program.

Thank you to the team from Sunway Group for their continued support and the confidence that they have placed in us—Dr. Jeffrey Cheah, Founder and Chairman of Sunway Group; Dr. See-Yan Lin, President of the Harvard Club of Malaysia; Dr. Weng Keng Lee, CEO of Education and Healthcare Division; Dr. Elizabeth Lee,

Senior Executive Director of the Sunway Education Group; Ms. Ng Beng Lean, Director of the Office of the Senior Executive Director of the Sunway Education Group; and the administrative staff.

My sincere gratitude goes to Ms. Ida Fazila Ismail, Head of Acumen Case Center at CALI Malaysia for her diligence and valuable contributions to overseeing the writing style and quality of the book content.

Last but not least, I wish to express my utmost appreciation to my hardworking team at CALI Boston, Ms. Ursula DeYoung, Advisor of Publication Affairs; and CALI Malaysia—Dr. Gin Chee Tong, Head of Strategy and Management; Ms. Jocelyn Lew En Mei, Strategy and Management Executive; Ms. Farzeera Emir, Executive Assistant to President; and the Center's interns, Michelle S Lee and Serena Kaan Tsu Li for their patience and professionalism in ensuring the successful completion of the book.

Words cannot express my heartfelt appreciation for their support, understanding, and contribution to the project. Thank you, everyone.

| Appendix I |

Program Details

● ● ●

1. Personal Leadership: Ethics, Power, and Decision Making
&
2. Case Method Teaching: A Way Forward for Effective Pedagogy

A. Plenary Sessions

The 90-minute sessions will engage participants in in-depth discussions on actual cases to develop in them moral competence and practical ethical judgement.

Plenary A. *Professor Kenneth Winston*
Day 1: A Framework for Professional Ethics
Day 2: Personal Convictions and Public Decision Making
Day 3: The Ethics of Obedience & Dissent
Day 4: Ethics in a Non-Ideal World
Day 5: The Ethics of Exercising Power

Plenary B. *Professor Mathias Risse*
Day 1: Our Common Humanity
Day 2: Taking Each Person Seriously
Day 3: More on Lying versus Deception
Day 4: Operating in a Flawed System
Day 5: Ethics and Leadership

B. Study Group Session

Led by Harvard Teaching Fellows, these 50-minute exercises are for participants to discuss the previous day's materials for a richer experience, and to debrief on expectation for the present day's cases. Participants are expected to come to class having read through the cases assigned, and with questions for a robust discussion.

C. Case Teaching & Practice

Led by Professor Kenneth Winston, in the 90-minute sessions, participants will learn how to develop a teaching and learning model that encourages debates, reflection, and a sharpening of reasoning and critical thinking skills. Participants will also learn case writing that are applicable and relevant to the needs of their students and the school.

D. Small Group Case Discussion

Led by the Harvard Teaching Fellows, the 90-minute exercises will provide participants with the opportunity for intimate discussions on personal stories and critique of them. They will also be guided on how to scrutinize, evaluate and learn from ethical issues that may arise in their professional lives.

E. Workshops

Entrepreneurship in Practice: Creating Shared Values
Panche Kralev

When we think of entrepreneurship, we think of starting a business. But entrepreneurship begins as a way of thinking strategically about any challenge. This has been the starting point on how the most successful entrepreneurs have developed the most innovative solutions to the world's most pressing problems. In this workshop, students will engage in case study discussions and lectures to build contextualized and experiential knowledge in aspects of entrepreneurship: mission and vision, positioning, funding, and resources as well as impact and measurement. Crucially, participants will develop relevant skillsets in these areas through hands-on activities and simulations. At the end of this workshop, participants will be better equipped to approach and lead a new entrepreneurial venture as an independent startup or within a large organization.

Leadership Communications: Cross-Cultural Competencies
Randy Tarnowski

Navigating groups and teams across cultural boundaries is critical for success in virtually any field, particularly in our increasingly globalized world. Whether the challenge arises from differences along ethnic, organizational, or national lines – individuals are needed to employ successful strategies to bridge differences and help diverse groups make progress on collective challenges. In the context of this workshop, we will view cross cultural leadership as a process. Participants will acquire a deeper understanding of culture as norms, become more adept at approaching and diagnosing challenges that arise from differences in culture and values, as well as practice cross-cultural competencies through social learning exercises.

Personal Leadership: From Purpose to Action
Lisa Lee

In a world full of vision, strategy and goals that are regularly being cast for organizations, businesses, governments, and the world, we too need a personal vision and plan of action for our own lives in order to find purpose, fulfilment, and personal success. This workshop is focused on defining and clarifying your own personal purpose and translating that into actionable strategy for your current life stage. Participants will learn how to assess opportunities, evaluate options, hedge oneself against risk, and develop an action plan that works for them. By learning the tools to identify what one wants to accomplish and evaluate multiple courses of that can lead to purpose fulfillment- you will walk away with the self-confidence needed to succeed.

F. Professional Development

These study group sessions are designed to advance participants' ancillary capabilities in verbal, written, and professional areas by providing them with knowledge, best practices, and skillsets that will help them in their personal, academic, and professional life.

- Communication Skills, *Lisa Lee*
- Authentic Leadership, *Panche Kralev*
- Giving an Elevator Pitch, *Randy Tarnowski*

G. Special Talks

How is Your Mindset Affecting Your Ability to Lead?
Randy Tarnowski

Is your mindset affecting your ability to lead? At this talk, Randy Tarnowski discusses recent research which he and other Harvard University researchers have conducted on the relationship between social networks and growth mindset. He presents four important advantages for leaders in business, education, and politics in instilling a growth mindset in your team.

Practicing Authentic Leadership
Lisa Lee

To find meaningful purpose, one must understand the most important values that are governing your life. In this talk, Lisa will share her own personal journey of how she changed from approaching people and problems from the way they are to what they could be. She will share how to take action based on your values and how that translates into authentic leadership.

H. Schedule

	MON	TUE	WED	THU	FRI
7:00am	Registration	Preparation and Breakfast			Breakfast
8:00am	Welcoming Ceremony & Orientation	Study Group Session			
8:50am		Plenary Session A			
10:20am		Tea Break			
10:50am		Plenary Session B			

12:20pm	Lunch Break				Lunch & Prayers
1:10pm	Case Teaching & Practice / Small Group Case Discussion				Group Presentation (1:30pm)
2:40pm	Tea Break				Tea Break (3:00pm)
3:00pm	Workshops				Workshops (3:20pm)
4:20pm	Professional Development	Special Talks	Professional Development	Panel Discussion	Debriefing and Comment (4:40pm)
5:00pm	Networking & End of Day				Break (5:10pm)
5:40pm					Award Ceremony & Graduation Dinner

3. Community Leadership: Leading Change for Organizational Renewal

A. Plenary Sessions

The 80-minute sessions will provide participants with the frameworks to become effective change agents in a dynamic, shifting, and interdependent world.

> Plenary A: Building High-Impact Teams: Fostering Entrepreneurial Mindsets at Work
> Plenary B: Constructive Collaboration: Creating a Team-Oriented Environment
> Plenary C: Power and Influence: Achieving Shared Goals and Objectives
> Plenary D: Leadership Communication: Becoming a Trusted Advisor
> Plenary E: What it Means to be a "Global Change Agent"
> Plenary F: The Distinction between Power, Authority and Leadership, and Why This Matters
> Plenary G: Diagnose Key "Adaptive Challenges
> Plenary H: Focus on Interventions to Mobilize People to Do Adaptive Work and Generate "Breakthrough Results"
> Plenary I: The Change Agent as Context Manager for Adaptive Work
> Plenary J: The Boundary Work of Leadership
> Plenary K: Leading Creatively

Plenary L: The Personal Work of Leadership: Being Responsible for "Self" as an Instrument of Power

B. Seminar

In these 50-minute seminars, participants will learn the skills and strategies for effective communication to make a positive impact at the workplace. They will also be exposed to useful traits on managing group dynamics, and be guided on how to motivate and engage key stakeholders to work toward a shared goal.

Seminar A: Leadership Communication: Inspiring the Team
Seminar B: Leadership Communication: The Power of Dialogue

C. Schedule

	MON	TUES	WED
8:00am		Registration/ Breakfast	
9:00am	Plenary A	Plenary E	Plenary I
10:20am		Tea Break	
10:40am	Plenary B	Plenary F	Plenary J
12:00pm		Lunch	
1:00pm	Plenary C	Plenary G	Plenary K
2:20pm		Tea Break	
2:40pm	Plenary D	Plenary H	Plenary L
4:00pm		Short Break	
4:10pm	Seminar A	Seminar B	Graduation Dinner
5:00pm		End	

| Appendix II |

About the Teaching Faculty

● ● ●

1. Personal Leadership: Ethics, Power, and Decision Making
&
2. Case Method Teaching: A Way Forward for Effective Pedagogy

Kenneth Winston, *Retired Lecturer in Ethics at the Ash Center for Democratic Governance and Innovation, Harvard Kennedy School*

Kenneth Winston taught practical and professional ethics at HKS from 1986 to 2015 and served as faculty chair of the HKS Singapore Program from 2008 to 2015. Winston has written extensively on case teaching, professional ethics, and legal theory.

His most recent book is *Ethics in Public Life: Good Practitioners in a Rising Asia* (2015). He co-edited *Prospects for the Professions in China* (2011) and edited *The Principles of Social Order: Selected Essays of Lon L. Fuller* (rev. ed. 2001). Winston has been a fellow of the American Council of Learned Societies, a senior research fellow of the

National Endowment for the Humanities, and a John Dewey senior fellow. He lives in Cambridge with his wife, Mary Jo Bane, and enjoys hiking, birding, and cooking.

Mathias Risse, *Professor of Philosophy and Public Policy at Harvard Kennedy School*

Mathias Risse works mostly in social and political philosophy, and in ethics. His primary research areas are contemporary political philosophy, in particular questions of international justice, distributive justice, human rights, and property.

In 2012, he published two books on questions of global justice, *On Global Justice* (Princeton University Press), which sets out his own proposal for how to think about justice at the global level; and *Global Political Philosophy* (MacMillan), which is a text book introduction to the field of political philosophy that focuses on ethical questions about globalization. Both books combine foundational philosophical inquiry with relatively applied questions about immigration, climate change, obligations to future generations, institutional reform at the global level, and human rights.

Risse studied philosophy, mathematics, and mathematical economics at the University of Bielefeld, the University of Pittsburgh, the Hebrew University of Jerusalem, and Princeton University. He received his BA, BS, and MS in mathematics from Bielefeld, and his MA and PhD in philosophy from Princeton. Before coming to Harvard, he taught in the Department of Philosophy and the Program in Ethics, Politics, and Economics at Yale.

Appendix II | About the Teaching Faculty

Hungsoo S. Kim, *MPA, Harvard Kennedy School*

Hungsoo S. Kim is the Co-founder and President of the Center for Asia Leadership Initiatives. Passionate about nurturing and empowering talents in Asia, he has developed and organized over twenty-five programs in more than twenty-two countries in the region to help budding leaders enhance their leadership competencies to navigate challenges in the 21st century. Hungsoo aims to engage with youth in all forty-eight countries in Asia by 2022 and inspire them to enact change in the world.

John Lim, *Tufts Fletcher School; Harvard Extension School*

John Lim is Co-founder and Managing Director of CALI Boston. A former fellow of the Harvard University Asia Center, he has worked in diverse organizations including the Embassy of Canada in Korea, the International Crisis Group, and in different sectors such as English education and social entrepreneurship. His current work engages him in researching and applying various leadership, education, and entrepreneurial models and frameworks within the Asian contexts.

Panche Kralev, *MCMPA, Harvard Kennedy School*

Panche Kralev is currently serving as President of the Board of Directors of Macedonian Telekom (Deutsche Telekom Group). He is a former Minister of Education and Science and Advisor to the Prime Minister of the Republic of Macedonia. During his career, he has also worked in investment banking, part of Raiffeisen Investment and the SEAF equity fund. Kralev is a former Mason Fellow of the MPA at the Harvard Kennedy School and brings insight into public policy, leadership, and strategy.

Lisa Lee, *Ed.M., Harvard Graduate School of Education*

Lisa Lee is a recent graduate of the Harvard Graduate School of Education, where she received her Master's degree in International Education Policy. She came to Harvard after teaching and consulting in Kazakhstan for nearly three years, where she started an initiative for university students to engage in critical issues in their immediate contexts. Previous to teaching, Lee worked on Wall Street as a global investment analyst and equity trader. Lee is a firm believer in taking all experiences at one's disposal and channeling them to make maximum impact. Her studies at Harvard focused on education and innovation, as well as entrepreneurial management. She founded the Harvard Graduate School of Education Progressive Education Network (PEN), a student organization aimed at forming meaningful networks of innovators who propel education forward. Through PEN, she launched Ed Harmony the first annual education innovation and networking showcase at the Harvard Innovation Lab. She is currently developing a 21st century skill curriculum and is passionate about education that empowers others to think critically and meaningfully about their role in the world around them. Lee's other passions include eating exotic foods, learning about different cultures, and discovering the good in people.

Randy Tarnowski, *Ed.M., Harvard Graduate School of Education*

Randy Tarnowski is a current Masters degree candidate at the Harvard Graduate School of Education. Previously, as Executive Assistant at the Korean-American Educational Commission, Randy managed the Fulbright Senior Scholar and Junior Researcher programs in order to foster cross-national partnerships. As Program Manager for

WorldTeach, Tarnowski supports international teaching programs in over thirteen countries. He is a previous recipient of the Fulbright grant to South Korea, as well as the Young Kil & Sunny Kim Scholarship from the Korean American Scholarship Foundation. In terms of research, Tarnowski is interested in the "internationalization" movement within higher education institutions and its implications on global equity. Tarnowski's written work can be found in a *Hard Questions on Global Educational Change* (Teachers College Press, 2016) and in *The Routledge Handbook for Global Child Welfare* (Routledge, 2016).

3. Community Leadership:
Leading Change for Organizational Renewal

Dean Williams, *Adjunct Lecturer in Public Policy for the Center for Public Leadership, Harvard Kennedy School*

Dean Williams teaches at Harvard University's Kennedy School and is based at the Center for Public Leadership. He is the faculty director of the Global Change Agent executive education program. He is the author of *Real Leadership: Helping People and Organizations Face Their Toughest Challenges* and *Leadership for a Fractured World: How to Cross Boundaries, Build Bridges, and Lead Change*.

Williams was the Chief Advisor to the President of Madagascar, helping the President orchestrate a dynamic process of national development. He was also the advisor to the government of East Timor in its early stages of independence. He has consulted and advised numerous companies, governments, and senior executives all over the world on leadership development and organizational change.

Hungsoo S. Kim, *MPA, Harvard Kennedy School*

Hungsoo S. Kim is the Co-founder and President of the Center for Asia Leadership Initiatives. Passionate about nurturing and empowering talents in Asia, he has developed and organized over twenty-five programs in more than twenty-two countries in the region to help budding leaders enhance their leadership competencies to navigate challenges in the 21st century. Hungsoo aims to engage with youth in all forty-eight countries in Asia by 2022 and inspire them to enact change in the world.

| Appendix III |

List of Contributors

•••

Introduction

Hungsoo S. Kim, *Korean*
President, Center for Asia Leadership Initiatives
MPA, Harvard Kennedy School of Government

•••

History and Philosophy

Hungsoo S. Kim, *Korean*
President, Center for Asia Leadership Initiatives
MPA, Harvard Kennedy School of Government

Dr. Gin Chee Tong, *Malaysian*
Head of Strategy & Management, CALI Malaysia

• • •

Case Method Teaching: A Way Forward for Effective Pedagogy

Dr. Cordelia Mason, *Malaysian*
Research Fellow of Strategy, Policy Development & Research, Asian Institute of Finance

Dr. Hendry Ng, *Malaysian*
Director of Victoria University Postgraduate Programmes, Sunway College

• • •

Personal Leadership: Ethics, Power, and Decision Making

Elma Berisha, *Kosovan*
General Manager of Strategy, Policy Development & Research, Asian Institute of Finance

Yasmin M. Handrich, *German*
Account Director, Kantar Worldpanel

Peter K.H. Law, *Malaysian*
Head of Talent Management & Learning & Development, Great Eastern Life Assurance (Malaysia) Berhad

Community Leadership: Leading Change for Organizational Renewal

Ida Fazila Ismail, *Malaysian*
Head of Acumen Case Center, CALI Malaysia

Sheikh Mohammed Irfan, *Bangladeshi*
Director of Admin-Research and Development at Cyber Giant

Shamza Khan, *Pakistani*
Case Writer and Author, Columbia and Harvard University

Katherine Kee, *Malaysian*
Manager of Public Relations, Sunway Education Group

www.ingramcontent.com/pod-product-compliance
Lightning Source LLC
Chambersburg PA
CBHW052347220526
45465CB00003BA/992